WALKI

SOUTHERN PENNINES

ROCHDALE | CANAL TRUST
MANCHESTER | SOWERBY BRIDGE
19 MILES | 13 MILES

Paul Hannon

HILLSIDE

HILLSIDE GUIDES - ACROSS THE NORTH AND BEYOND

Mountain Walking
•THE HIGH PEAKS OF ENGLAND & WALES

Long Distance Walks
•COAST TO COAST WALK   •DALES WAY   •CLEVELAND WAY
•WESTMORLAND WAY   •FURNESS WAY   •CUMBERLAND WAY
•LADY ANNE'S WAY   •PENDLE WAY   •NIDDERDALE WAY
•TRANS-PENNINE WAY   •NORTH BOWLAND TRAVERSE

Hillwalking - Lake District
•LAKELAND FELLS - SOUTH   •LAKELAND FELLS - EAST
•LAKELAND FELLS - NORTH   •LAKELAND FELLS - WEST

Circular Walks - Peak District
•NORTHERN PEAK   •EASTERN PEAK   •CENTRAL PEAK
• SOUTHERN PEAK   •WESTERN PEAK

Circular Walks - Yorkshire Dales
•HOWGILL FELLS   •THREE PEAKS   •MALHAMDALE
•WHARFEDALE   •NIDDERDALE   •WENSLEYDALE   •SWALEDALE
•FREEDOM OF THE DALES

Circular Walks - North York Moors
•WESTERN MOORS   •SOUTHERN MOORS   •NORTHERN MOORS

Circular Walks - South Pennines
•BRONTE COUNTRY   •ILKLEY MOOR
•CALDERDALE   •SOUTHERN PENNINES

Circular Walks - Lancashire
•BOWLAND   •PENDLE & THE RIBBLE   •WEST PENNINE MOORS

Circular Walks - North Pennines
•TEESDALE   •EDEN VALLEY

Yorkshire Pub Walks
•HARROGATE/WHARFE VALLEY   •HAWORTH/AIRE VALLEY

Biking Guides
•YORKSHIRE DALES CYCLE WAY   •WEST YORKSHIRE CYCLE WAY
•MOUNTAIN BIKING - WEST & SOUTH YORKSHIRE
•AIRE VALLEY BIKING GUIDE   •CALDERDALE BIKING GUIDE
•GLASGOW Clyde Valley & Loch Lomond

•YORK WALKS *City Theme Walks*

Send for a detailed current catalogue and pricelist

SOUTHERN PENNINES

Paul Hannon

HILLSIDE

HILLSIDE
PUBLICATIONS
12 Broadlands
Shann Park
Keighley
West Yorkshire
BD20 6HX

First published 1999

© Paul Hannon 1999

ISBN 1 870141 68 7

Cover illustrations: Eastergate Bridge, Marsden;
Haigh Clough, beneath the Buckstones
Back cover: Saddleworth Edges; Tunnel End, Marsden;
Aiggin Stone, Blackstone Edge; Holmfirth
(Paul Hannon/Big Country Picture Library)

Page 1: On the Rochdale Canal
Page 3: Bishop Park monument, Grains Bar

Printed in Great Britain by
Carnmor Print & Design
95-97 London Road
Preston
Lancashire
PR1 4BA

CONTENTS

INTRODUCTION

The South Pennines is a vast area reaching from the Aire Gap to Black Hill, from the Yorkshire Dales National Park to the Peak District National Park. Within its bounds are numerous individual areas, with Calderdale at its heart, and Brontë Country further north. To the south of Calderdale is the area of this guide, the southernmost quarter of the South Pennines. Here the Pennines form a better defined watershed than further north, emphatically splitting the settlements on either side. Conversely, however, they are also well linked by a veritable plethora of transport routes from down the centuries, culminating in the M62 motorway.

The Southern Pennines simply ooze character, borne in no small way out of the Industrial Revolution. Even seemingly far from the milltowns that were at the heart of that sweeping change, one is never far from its evidence, be it reservoirs, old quarries, turnpike roads, canals or packhorse trails, as well as hamlets where handloom weaving thrived in beautiful three-storeyed houses of which many survive. Reservoirs ensured a water supply for growing towns, be it for drinking water or the textile mills, and also to keep the canals topped up with this precious if not entirely rare commodity. Earlier, the fast-flowing water in the deep cloughs kept the waterwheels of older mills turning.

On the Yorkshire side, two principal valleys run parallel courses out through the hills to Huddersfield, with the Holme Valley focused on Holmfirth and the Colne Valley on Marsden. To the west, a more complicated arrangement of hills and dales is based around the upper reaches of the river Tame, with the cultural centre of Saddleworth very much at the heart. Despite what modern maps may claim, Saddleworth is true Yorkshire, a little corner of God's Own Country that crept over the Pennines but since 1974 has been mischievously purloined. The environs of Littleborough offer further interest to the north.

Such is the northerly march of the Peak District that a number of these walks reach within its bounds, though there is an undeniable 'Pennine' rather than 'Peak' feel to the surrounds. The backbone of the Southern Pennines reaches from Black Hill to Blackstone Edge, which with Millstone Edge and Windy Hill are suitable names to convey something of the nature of these wild hills. Perhaps the most constant reminders of man's influence, even more than drystone walls, are the reservoirs, and very few walks do not encounter them in some shape or form.

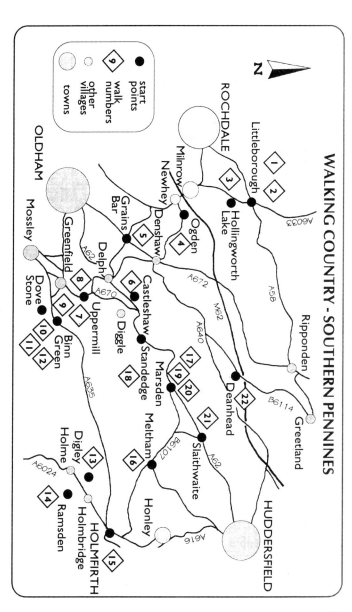

WALKING COUNTRY - SOUTHERN PENNINES

Legend:
- start points
- walk numbers
- other villages
- towns

7

Access

While the vast majority of the walking is on rights of way, sections of some walks take advantage of other formal arrangements. Two walks make use of agreements negotiated by the Peak National Park: both begin from Dove Stone Reservoir in Chew Valley, and though largely on rights of way, they also cross access land which can be closed on occasional days of shooting and at times of high fire risk (rights of way are not affected). Boundaries of access land are marked on Outdoor Leisure maps. Numerous other walks use canal towpaths or permissive paths. Please obey any legitimate signs encountered: rights of way as well as other routes can be opened, closed or diverted. On such occasions, official notices take precedence over the guidebook.

Getting around

Set between some of the north's great conurbations, the area is highly accessible from most Yorkshire and Lancashire towns and cities. Within the area itself most settlements enjoy public transport links with the larger towns of Oldham, Rochdale and Huddersfield. Small towns such as Holmfirth, Marsden, Littleborough and Uppermill serve as focal points. All the walks begin within little more than a few miles of each other, all are on or near major roads, and virtually all can be reached by public transport, often by train as well as bus. With a little planning, many permutations can be created by linking sections of the walks, to create longer routes or to take advantage of transport.

Using the guide

Each walk is self-contained, essential information being followed by a simple map and a route description. In between are notes of features along the way, with illustrations to capture the flavour of the walks and record items of interest. To make the instructions easy to follow, essential route description is highlighted in bold type, while items in lighter type refer to historical asides and things to look out for: in this format you can find your way more easily while still locating features of interest at the relevant point. The sketch maps identify the location of routes rather than fine detail, and whilst the description should be sufficient to guide you around, an Ordnance Survey map is recommended. To gain the most from a walk, the detail of the 1:25,000 maps is unsurpassed. They also serve to vary walks as desired, giving an improved picture of one's surroundings and the availability of linking paths. Just two maps cover the walks in the book:-

•*Outdoor Leisure 1 - Peak District, Dark Peak; 21 - South Pennines*

Also useful for general planning are these two Landranger maps at 1:50,000 scale: *109, Manchester; 110, Sheffield & Huddersfield*

ROCHDALE CANAL

START Littleborough   Grid ref. SD 938163

DISTANCE 7 (or 5) miles

ORDNANCE SURVEY MAPS
1:50,000
Landranger 109 - Manchester
Landranger 103 - Blackburn & Burnley (tiny section)
1:25,000
Outdoor Leisure 21 - South Pennines

ACCESS Start from the Heritage Centre on Lodge Street just behind the parish church. Some street parking here or a little further afield. Served by bus and train from Rochdale and Halifax.

Though focused largely on the canal, this grand walk has much additional interest.

S For notes on Littleborough see WALK 2. **Return to Church Street outside the parish church on the main road junction.** Across the road stands a former toll-house dating from around 1824: there is a more interesting one to follow later. **Cross to the Halifax road, passing under the railway bridge. Turn right on Canal Street (B6225) to reach the Rochdale Canal, then go left on the towpath. At the first lock cross the bridge and quickly leave the canal by a snicket by a terrace of houses (Oak Street).** Don't worry, there is plenty of canal to come! Joining a lane bear right along it, beneath an extensive millpond up on the left and past Ealees Mill on the right. Becoming a broad drive it runs on into the greenery of the Ealees Valley.

After opening out a little, leave the track by a clear path branching left up to and over a long dried-up mill-cut in Ealees Wood. The short path rises to a small gate at the rear of the house at Lane Foot: don't use it, but turn uphill with the hedge. Again, ignore the main path passing through the hedge, and remain on its near side. In season this bank is decorated with bluebells. A much fainter path rises up the side of this well defined spur, which is not densely wooded as the OS map suggests. The way becomes a little clearer as it rises above some scrub to reveal a fence-stile at the top. Down to the left, Ealees millpond leads the eye to Littleborough's church spire; looking back the Ealees Valley leads to Hollingworth Lake, while due east is the craggy frown of Blackstone Edge.

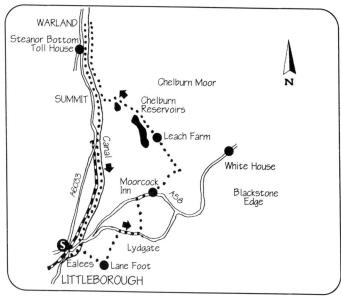

Resume up the field to a stile by the top right corner, then follow the wall away. Ahead is a view through the Summit Gap, while to the right the 'Roman' road descending from Blackstone Edge is very prominent. Ignoring a stile before a barn, advance to the far corner alongside a farm (obscured on map). From the gate keep left of all the buildings and a walled track rises to meet the drive above the house. Follow this out over the brow, becoming enclosed to debouch onto Blackstone Edge Old Road. Turn right on this over the brow and down to Lydgate. Just ahead, incidentally, is an attractive old mill-pond by the roadside.

Ignore the first path on the left, along a field edge, and go just yards further to one at a gate at the drive of Lydgate Manor. Follow the fence alongside the drive, then bear left down into the improved surrounds of Lydgate Clough. Here begins a charming stroll with the tiny meandering stream through a deep, hidden little valley. A novel little waterslide, several crossings of the stream, a tiny old water-cut, a small landslip and the site of an old dam all add to the interest. After the third stream crossing a stile sees the path runs on with the water-cut, then crossing it to climb stone steps to a stile onto the A58.

Cross and turn uphill to the *Moorcock Inn*. At the end of its car park bear left on a rough road, and keep straight on it to emerge onto the open moor. Turning left it forks: take the upper one which curves round to another fork at the side of the moor. Here go left, over Castle Clough to head away as an enclosed track past various outbuildings. Remain on the main track which ends at the white-walled Leach Farm. En route Higher Chelburn Reservoir appears in its odd location between Snoddle Hill and the main body of moorland, necessitating dams at both ends: nevertheless its setting is quite impressive, backed by the rough wall of Reddyshore Scout across the main valley.

Pass to the right of the buildings at Leach Farm, and beyond them a short enclosed way between old wall and fence leads to a pasture of tumbled boulders overlooking the reservoir. A path bears slightly left to a wall-stile hidden behind a boulder. It is immediately above here that the greater concentration of boulders can be found on Leach Hill, a fascinating jumble of dark gritstone in total disarray. The path runs down towards the end of the reservoir, but keeps well above it to cross a bridge over an inflowing channel, then on briefly with it before dropping more faintly down to join the access road.

The rough road leads down to the canal at Summit. En route it passes the much smaller Lower Chelburn Reservoir (both were built at the start of the 19th century to supply the Rochdale Canal), and gives good views over the Summit Gap, with several railway tunnel airshafts visible under Reddyshore Scout. Near the bottom, note the sizeable Mam Tor-like landslip on the hill just to our left. Just over the bridge is the A6033 Littleborough-Todmorden road, with the convenient attraction of the *Summit* pub. If taking the shorter route, then turn left on the towpath to return to Littleborough.

For the full walk, turn right up a rough road in front of a red-brick building just before the canal bridge. This rises a few yards to a rough crossroads, where turn left on a rough, level road heading away. When it climbs to a hairpin bend leave it for a stile on the left, and ignoring a grassy, ascending old quarry way, bear left towards the canal. An intermittent path runs on the base of the steep slope, and at a fork the left branch crosses to the canal bank at the foot of an old wall. Ahead, the rough wall of Reddyshore Scout impresses again.

Stride on here until reaching the scant remains of former buildings, with Steanor Bottom toll-house seen across the canal and road. Here bear right on a grassy old way rising to a house at Long Lees. Its drive then leads back down to the canal at Warland Upper Lock, the walk's turning point. A modern boundary stone by the swing bridge marks the divide between Yorkshire and Lancashire. If seeking refreshment, then follow the short lane out onto the A6033 at Warland Gate End to find the *Bird i'th' Hand* pub to your right.

Completed in 1804, the Rochdale Canal was the first of three trans-Pennine waterways. It runs for 33 miles from Manchester to the Calder & Hebble Navigation at Sowerby Bridge. Unlike the Huddersfield Narrow Canal (see page 78), it could take advantage of an extremely low level route across the Pennines, the Summit Gap. Nevertheless, earlier plans incorporated a 3000-yard tunnel, but the option of using locks proved more tempting. Over its full length some 92 were built, raising the waterway to an altitude of 600ft at its summit pool. This occurs between the next two locks encountered on the walk.

The demise of the canal began in 1841 when the Lancashire & Yorkshire Railway was completed, running a parallel course within a stone's throw of the towpath for many miles. Given the efficiency of the railways it is perhaps surprising that commercial traffic survived into the early decades of the 20th century. Long abandoned to nature and neglect, the canal has benefitted from splendid restoration work in recent years, all sparked by the formation of the fledgling Rochdale Canal Society in 1974. The final three miles require no instructions other than to turn left along the towpath to the lock where we joined the canal at Littleborough, and finish the walk as it began.

Features en route are numerous. The first lock is Longlees Lock, the highest on the Yorkshire side, then almost at once a stile gives access to a fieldside detour to the main road for a closer look at Steanor

Bottom Toll House. This stands on the old turnpike road (Calderbrook Road) as it comes back down to the valley. Happily the board advising the various tolls has been restored on the upper floor of this splendid reminder of travel in the past. Back on the towpath, modern county boundary signs are seen on the main road before reaching the first 'downhill' lock at Summit. This is the point where the shorter route comes in, and it may be worth a reminder that the *Summit* pub stands just a few yards up to the right.

As the walk resumes, a series of locks ensue, and a number of old mills and factories are soon encountered. Opposite a large mill we find an aqueduct on the right, carrying a stream over the railway line before it passes under the road just short of the Summit Tunnel entrance. The Summit Tunnel was the high point of the railway's trans-Pennine crossing, and at the time of its opening was the world's longest. More than a mile long, it was the scene of a major fire in 1984, when a set of petrol waggons derailed and set ablaze.

The surroundings become greener for a time before the railway comes alongside. A vehicle scrapyard makes a foreground to Littleborough church spire before passing deep under the A58 road bridge and back to Canal Street, and almost the end.

Steanor Bottom Toll House

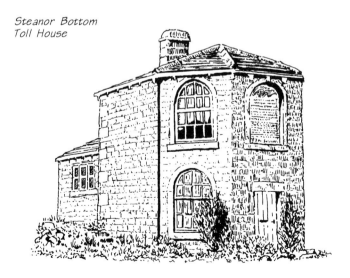

BLACKSTONE EDGE

2

START *Littleborough*   *Grid ref. SD 938163*

DISTANCE *9 miles*

ORDNANCE SURVEY MAPS
1:50,000
Landranger 109 - Manchester
1:25,000
Outdoor Leisure 21 - South Pennines

ACCESS *Start from the Heritage Centre on Lodge Street just behind the parish church. Some street parking here or a little further afield. Served by bus and train from Rochdale and Halifax.*

A fine ascent to the bracing heights of Blackstone Edge, one of the great South Pennine landmarks.

⑤   Littleborough is an independent little place perhaps best known for nearby Hollingworth Lake, but it is well positioned in its own right on the approach to the Summit Gorge leading through to Yorkshire. Making its unassuming way through is the river Roch, which of course gives its name to the large town which keeps Littleborough under its wing. The Rochdale Canal also flows within a stone's throw of the centre. Of great interest to visitors, and an ideal place from which to set forth into the local countryside, is the Heritage Centre located in the old Coach House: this is a 200 year old stabling block of the surviving *Falcon Inn*, restored in 1988, along with a coffee shop.

Return to Church Street outside the parish church on the main road junction. Across the road stands a former toll-house dating from around 1824. **Cross to the Halifax road, passing under the railway bridge. Turn right on Canal Street (B6225) to reach the Rochdale Canal, then go left on the towpath.** For a note on the Rochdale Canal see page 12. **At the first lock cross the bridge and quickly leave the canal by a snicket by a terrace of houses (Oak Street). Keep straight on at the end to join a lane. Bear right on this, beneath an extensive millpond on the left and past Ealees Mill on the right. Becoming a broad drive it runs on into the greenery of the Ealees Valley.**

Keep on past a branch left up over a long dried-up mill-cut: the walk concludes over this. A little further is a path junction as the drive swings up to the left. Cross the tiny stream in front and straight up the broad path in front, ignoring the branch right that stays with the main beck. Rise by the fence and then left up to the corner of the field. Don't take the stile by the gate but turn down to the right to another corner. Through the stile go straight on with the wall, over another stile and along the field-side. Beyond a prominent tree cross a farm bridge and bear left up to the field corner. A firm track is joined rising left to Brearley. Hollingworth Lake is seen to the right.

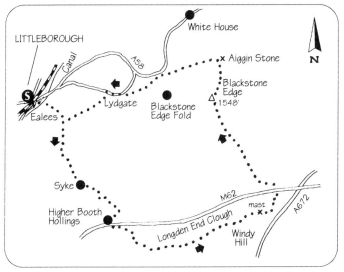

Pass to the right of the buildings to arrive at the old drain. This was built to carry water from Hollingworth Lake to the canal. **Cross it and turn left to follow this pleasantly away beneath Hollingworth Hill, continuing on past the drain's demise to join a firm track just short of Syke House.** Over to the left are the slag heaps of abandoned small-scale coal workings, while the drone of the M62 traffic is already audible. **Turn right on the track then left up the front of the house, a good track rising along the moor edge. Ignoring lesser branches, this rises to a gate in a corner on the right. Don't go through, but faithfully follow a zigzag that doubles back across towards the wall on the right to resume uphill more directly.** There are now good views back over Hollingworth Lake and Littleborough to lonely moors to the north, while Blackstone Edge dominates closer to hand.

At the top a harder track is met, and turning right the M62 finally appears. The track drops down to a gate then down a field to Higher Booth Hollings Farm. Pass along the front and out on its drive, which crosses the motorway by a high bridge. Looking east, the Pennine Way footbridge and Windy Hill mast sit on the hilltop: not quite the summit of our walk, but by then most of the climbing will be over.

Across the motorway, turn left on the old road which runs on to enter a field. Slant down a grass track to the right to a gateway by a ruin. Pass through and bear left along the front of the extensive ruins. On the opposite side of the clough, our route to the moortop is identified by a string of such ruins. **The green track runs on a little further, crossing a stream before we descend beyond reedy pools to a kissing-gate and thence a stone bridge over Longden End Brook. Ignore the track heading away and climb the bank to meet another broad track. Cross straight over and up to the left of another ruin. Just behind is an old path, go left on this above a spoil heap and beneath a fenced water enclosure to rejoin the track. This rises into a small clough before crossing it. The track then runs on for some time across the rough pasture.** Down below is Longden End Clough, though it is a lengthy section of the M62 across it that holds the attention.

Rising ever gently the track leads to a forlorn ruin, beyond which it fades. Locate the next ruin ahead and contour to it across mixed ground. Note that an alternative doubles back from here, the grassy old drive slanting back up to the skyline where it meets Tunshill Lane (see WALK 4) on the ridgetop: that walk also leads to the Windy Hill mast. **The main route heads off on a faint way, again making for a ruin (Windy Hill) further along. Once more a largely pathless gentle rise leads on through an old wall, beyond which a good green way runs on to this more substantial ruin. A sunken way rises behind it to a knoll, then up a clear track onto the brow of Windy Hill.** Blackstone Edge is now looking impressive above the motorway.

Remain on the track through a gateway and along to the perimeter fence of the mast, where passing to the left an access road is met. Go right to meet the main access road, then left out on this to cross the Pennine Way. Ahead, the M62 runs purposefully on into Yorkshire. Just over to the right on the summit of the A672, the Pennine Way leads to a snack bar. **The route turns left on the firm path of the PW to drop down to cross the M62 footbridge.**

This is a rare chance to be the highest person in the country 'on' a motorway, and perched 65ft above the speeding traffic one can't but help feel superior. **Across, bear left on the broad path heading away, soon swinging around to the right to replace the M62 with the prospect of Blackstone Edge, a fair deal!** This splendidly restored path will come as a major shock to anyone with grim memories of its predecessor across the peat bogs of Redmires. **With the bouldery crest of the edge straight ahead, the path leads unerringly up to its top. The edge itself actually forms well before the waymarked path reaches it, and many obviously make for its attractions when the path is just yards short of the edge. At 1548ft/472m the highest point is not in doubt, as an Ordnance Survey column is cemented securely to a mighty boulder.**

Blackstone Edge is overtopped only by the Saddleworth Edges (WALK 11) and West Nab on Meltham Moor (WALK 16) in this collection of walks. The view is outstanding, though perhaps the finest feature is the rocky edge itself. Westwards we look down on a spread of greater Manchester beyond Littleborough and Hollingworth Lake. The Summit Gorge leads the eye to Coal Clough windfarm and Pendle Hill through the Cliviger Gorge, while to the north Black Hameldon and Boulsworth Hill lead round to Ovenden Moor windfarm. Southwards are the high moors of the Dark Peak. The finest climbing amongst what is otherwise largely scrambling opportunities is found towards the northern limits of the edge, a short way down the slope: this massive cliff presents bold faces and one or two interesting chimneys.

Resume northwards along the edge path, soon crossing more modest stony ground to a gate admitting onto the old road at the Aiggin Stone. At this important junction of packhorse routes the Rochdale-Halifax and Oldham-Burnley trails met. Remarkably there is more of this restored ancient waymarker below ground than above. **Turn left down the broad track, soon encountering the superb surviving paved section.**

Long thought to be of Roman origin, it is now generally attributed to more recent times, for in 1735 this became the first turnpike road in the area. Of particular interest and curiosity is the grooved channel in the centre. Certainly this route was used by the Romans, and also later as a major trans-Pennine packhorse route linking Halifax and Rochdale, though in this section the packhorse road wound a little further north: it too can be clearly discerned for much of its course. **This leads down across a water drain then delightfully down the moor, the paving remaining for a considerable time.** Looking back up to the edge, note the prominent climbing crags.

At the bottom cross over a farm drive without joining the A58, and resume down a wall-side path on the moor edge down to Lydgate. Keep straight on past the houses to emerge onto Blackstone Edge Old Road. This name explains all, for this is the original turnpike road of the 1760s, superseded by the present A58 about thirty years later. **Head along the road, passing an attractive old pond and a grouping that includes a former inn and mill. Just beyond, take a stile on the left and follow a faint track bearing left over the field to the far corner. From the stile remain with the right-hand wall through two fields to drop down to Owlet Hall.**

A tiny stream between two stiles is crossed, then pass to the right of the attractive, dark gritstone house. Don't take the forward gate onto the golf course, but the ornate one on the right. Head away above a wooded stream in the enchanting environs of the little Ealees Valley. The path crosses and then shadows an old millcut for a while. It also diverges with a lower branch dropping towards the stream before they rejoin to run on to a footbridge over it. Advance to the house at Lane Foot, rising to a little knoll to its right. Here the path doubles back down to the right to cross the earlier mill-cut nearer the start of the walk. Turn right to conclude as we began.

On Blackstone Edge

3

HOLLINGWORTH LAKE

START *Hollingworth Lake*   *Grid ref. SD 939152*

DISTANCE *3½ miles*

ORDNANCE SURVEY MAPS
1:50,000
Landranger 109 - Manchester
1:25,000
Outdoor Leisure 21 - South Pennines

ACCESS *Start from the Visitor Centre car park on the lake's east side, just off the B6225. There are other car parks on the B6225. Served by bus from Littleborough and Rochdale. Train station at Smithy Bridge, half a mile off route, served from Rochdale and Halifax.*

Hollingworth Lake is a long established and popular resort, with a wealth of nearby paths ensuring a more rewarding walk than merely the obvious circuit.

S The visitor centre opened in 1976, hard on the heels of the lake's designation as a country park. **From the Centre head down to the far end of the well landscaped car park.** Blackstone Edge occupies the skyline ahead. **Continue beyond the car park on a broad track, which quickly swings right after a pond to cross Hollingworth Brook and climb to a farm. Don't follow it but go straight ahead on a footpath liberally endowed with flags. This same pleasant and popular path leads on through several stiles/gates, crossing the brook part-way on.**

At the end, as the path is just about to join the drive to the white house at Lane Foot in front, double sharply back up to the right on a broad green path. Our goal is the hamlet of Whittaker, just above. The path rises to a stile by a gate, then slants up the field, crossing the canal drain en route. The lake reveals itself over to the right, though there will shortly be far better views of it. **The path continues**

up to a gap-stile in a rising wall, then up to a wall at the top. Ignore the stile in it and continue on to the end, through a gate and up into Whittaker. This former handloom weaving hamlet features a number of renovated houses, some dating back several centuries.

Rise up the cobbled road between the buildings, and when it turns sharp left to become surfaced behind the golf clubhouse, instead turn down to the right on a flagged path across a garden. Avoiding the lawn as directed, this swings round beneath the house to a gate above. A path slants down to another gate to the top of a wood, then drops through the trees to bridge the canal drain and leave the wood behind. At this path junction go straight ahead on the drainside path. By a stile at the end the drain has gone, and a firm track is joined. All around are slag heaps from former small-scale coal mining.

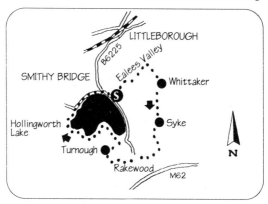

Advance along the track to approach the house at Syke, and leave the track to turn up the front of the houses. At the end turn right through a gate and up a steep walled track. At the top this offers the finest view of the lake, and the M62 is dramatically revealed on its stilts of the 140ft high Rakewood Viaduct. The rounded hill we are skirting is none other than Benny Hill, TV funnyman of the 1970s! Cross over the field to a gateway, then bear left to drop down to a ladder-stile in the corner. Go forward just a few yards to the next stile, then cross a partly reedy pasture, rising slightly to meet a track alongside a crumbling wall. Turn right on this bridleway to descend to Schofield Hall. Little now remains of this 16th century house that had survived to the turn of the 20th century.

Go down past the house, through a gate and down an old lane to emerge onto a road at Rakewood. Go left a few yards, past some three-storeyed cottages then right on the sports club drive. Leave before the car park by a snicket on the right, a level path that emerges onto the base of a hill at the end. Turn right on a part-sunken old way up the fence-side. At a sharp bend left, leave by a stile in the wall corner, and with a caravan site below head off on a broad green path slanting down to a stile/gate onto a drive. Cross straight over and down to meet a broad track, continuing up it towards Turnough Farm.

Without entering the farm take a stile on the right and cross to join a wall. Take a stile to its top side part way along, and as the path continues round the base of Turnough Hill, turn down to a kissing-gate just after the caravan site. A path runs on through a part wetland nature reserve. This quickly emerges onto the lake's circular path. For an emergency finish go right, otherwise join the weekend crowds and head left along the broad path. Passing a bird-hide it quickly opens up along the lakeside, curving round to reach the Promontory. Here are cafe, toilets and children's play area, though in Hollingworth Lake's heyday you could also have enjoyed a dance at the Lake Hotel, now but a distant memory.

Hollingworth Lake was long known as the 'Weighver's Seaport', such was its attraction to trippers of the Victorian era. The place was a hugely popular resort for millworkers for whom the real seaside was a long way. The attractions on their doorstep included boating, swimming, fishing, a 'Promenade', hotels, cafes, and amusements. A steam ferry operated too, and today a ferry still plies the lake, while modern day watersports are practised by many. The lake itself dates back two centuries, having been created to help supply the Rochdale Canal.

Continue round past a boat club and a ferry landing, and trace this same path all the way round to the road. Turn right along the Blackpool-like scene, passing several refreshment opportunities including the *Beach Hotel* before regaining the lakeshore after a car park. The last five minutes lead back to the *Fishermans* pub and then right to return to the car park entrance.

4

WHITE HILL

START Ogden   Grid ref. SD 952122

DISTANCE 8½ miles

ORDNANCE SURVEY MAPS
1:50,000
Landranger 109 - Manchester
Landranger 110 - Sheffield & Huddersfield (tiny section)
1:25,000
Outdoor Leisure 21 - South Pennines

ACCESS Start from Ogden Reservoir car park, on the easily missed Waterworks Road off the A640 a mile east of Newhey. Rochdale–Uppermill buses on the A640, and trains at Newhey.

A bracing walk typical of the region: largely on open moorland but laced with reservoirs in deep valleys.

S Ogden Reservoir is the lowest of no less than six that flood the Piethorne Valley: a glut of water even by Pennine catchment standards. They were built during the second half of the 19th century to supply Oldham and Rochdale. Before starting, a visit to the toilet is recommended to unearth some local information! **From the car park climb to the dam and cross to the far side. Rise to join a broad path and follow it to the right outside the base of a plantation.**

Having swung away from the reservoir, the path forks at a corner. Turn down to the right across a tiny stream and rise to rebuilt walling at a ruin. Rising left a broad track is joined. Bearing left this rises over rough pasture to a crossroads with a walled lane (the path actually veers off the track to join the lane further left). Ahead is a first glimpse of the pulsating M62, soon seen more impressively as it crosses the 140ft high Rakewood Viaduct high above Longden End Brook.

Turn right on the old sunken way of Tunshill Lane. With an attendant path avoiding sunken marshy sections, it rises for a good half-mile to swing round to a junction at Turf Hill Nick. Double back left on an inviting green way that resumes up the ridge. Our objective of the Windy Hill mast appears ahead, and not a great deal higher. Gradually emerging from walls it rises unfailingly onto the upper ridge. A long section of motorway is in view over to the left beneath the skyline of Blackstone Edge, while there are sweeping views east to the moorland topped by our imminent high point, White Hill.

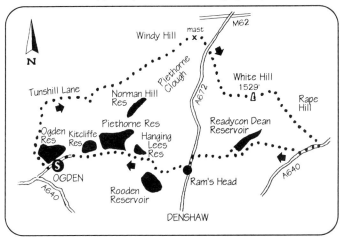

When the final wall at last expires at a gateway in a crumbling crosswall, a clear path continues, parting from the unused sunken way as it climbs to the waiting mast. The path runs left of its enclosure to join a broader track, which itself joins a firm access track alongside the mast. Turn right on this to the mast's access road, and left on it for a few yards only to intersect the Pennine Way. Go right to the summit of the A672 Oldham-Halifax road. Two features of varying interest here are an old boundary stone and an opportunity for refreshment with the truckers.

Cross straight over the road and head up the PW back onto the moor. A good firm section precedes a peaty one as the path curves up to the Ordnance Survey column surmounting White Hill. At 1529ft/ 466m this is the summit of the walk. To the north is Blackstone Edge, while rolling moorland views to the south feature the high moors of Bleaklow behind Black Hill and the Holme Moss mast. **Resume on the pleasant path as it drops towards the saddle at the head of Readycon Dean. En route it enters the National Trust's Marsden Moor estate at a stile and a repaired path takes over to cross the saddle. On the brow beyond, an old wall joins in as a swift descent is made to the A640.** Over to the left the road is seen running across the moor to Buckstones: ahead are Pule Hill and West Nab on Meltham Moor. To the left of the Emley Moor TV mast, almost touching the skyline is the tower on Castle Hill above Huddersfield.

Turn right for a few minutes only: this is a much quieter road than the last, and supports a nice verge on the other side. At the first chance take a right of way on the right at a gate and stile. A smashing old track initially rises then runs on into a seemingly untainted bowl in the hills. We are now on the historic Rapes Highway, a splendid old packhorse route linking Marsden and Milnrow (see also page 82). **Enjoy this section before Readycon Dean Reservoir appears in front, and the track descends to run along the reservoir wallside to the dam. Cross and head away on the track which quickly rises to meet the A672 again. Again with a verge, go briefly left to the inviting** *Rams Head* **pub above Denshaw.**

Immediately above the pub a firm track runs on past various outbuildings. After some sheep pens two parallel drives run down to the left. Take the second one, but across the cattle-grid leave it by slanting down the large field to a stile in the fence just short of the far corner. En route, Rooden Reservoir lies immediately ahead, with long views north-west to Rochdale and the moors to its north. **Descend to cross the Rooden Catchwater and down again to join a track.**

At the bigger track junction below, go left just a few yards then take an inviting path slanting up the knoll on the left. It rounds the end and affords a fine view over the Piethorne Valley. Beyond a stile the path runs down to a crossroads. Go right a few yards then on again with a reedy ditch to run down to join a hard track alongside Piethorne Reservoir. Head left on this to the end, where a surfaced road leads out past reservoir buildings and then cottages to return to the start.

5

DENSHAW SKYLINE

START *Grains Bar*   *Grid ref. SD 962085*

DISTANCE *7 miles*

ORDNANCE SURVEY MAPS
1:50,000
Landranger 109 - Manchester
1:25,000
Outdoor Leisure 1 - Peak District, Dark Peak
Outdoor Leisure 21 - South Pennines

ACCESS *Start from the Bishop Park car park on the A672, just west of the road junction at Grains Bar. Served by buses from Oldham, Rochdale, Halifax and Huddersfield. Shaw railway station is 1½ miles away. An alternative start is the busy junction at the heart of Denshaw, on the route.*

❺ Grains Bar is a meeting place of roads on a lofty hilltop, and at 1115ft/340m this is a windswept spot to find a pitch & putt course. It manages two pubs, and is a handy base for the popular Bishop Park and its monument, which with its extensive views is saved for the end of the walk. **At the central crossroads take a footpath signed within a yard of the roadsign, along the B6197 Shaw/Rochdale road (Buckstones Road), across the road from the *Bulls Head*. After a few yards parallel with the main A672 road it swings left to pass between gardens, then continues as a pleasant enclosed way. Part way on a stile transfers us into the field on the right, to continue on.** Ahead are extensive views to an endless Pennine skyline.

Over an intervening stile the way soon returns over the wall, continuing on to join an enclosed grassy way. Advance along this to a lone house, and continue on the gently rising way which narrows and becomes firmer underfoot. This proves a super tramp as it runs

along a well defined crest. It enjoys grand views to the right, over the upper Tame Valley and Saddleworth into the Chew Valley enclosed by the Saddleworth Edges, with Pots & Pans obelisk also prominent.

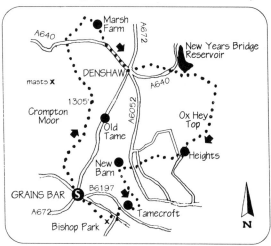

Passing beneath the power lines the route emerges into the open briefly, climbing White Hill by the wallside and soon becoming enclosed by old walls to emerge onto the crest of Crompton Moor. Looking down on Denshaw, New Year's Bridge Reservoir is seen behind it. **Forge straight on this rough moorland in the company of the right-hand wall. The highest point is innoccuously crossed at 1305ft/398m.** Over to the left across a hollow is a communications station on Crow Knowl, with views to the Lancashire Pennines far to the north-west, and Winter Hill with its great mast prominent still further left. **Maintain this course all the way along, gradually declining above Boothstead Edge to ultimately join the masts' access road at a gate on a bend. This drops down to meet the A640 Huddersfield-Rochdale road on a brow, with a former pub opposite.** Refreshment opportunities are still available just down to the right, however.

Cross straight over and along the rough road opposite. At its early junction turn right to Edge Gate, passing along the rear of the houses and away along a more inviting grassy track. Approaching Rooden Reservoir, look out for a hurdle-stile on the right, where a fence and old wall drop away. If missed, you'll soon reach a kissing-gate and emergence by a sturdy wall, so you know you've gone too far. **Descend the fence-side to another stile, and down a rougher enclosed way to a stile into a garden at Marsh Farm. Advance straight down its drive back onto the A640. Turn left along the footway for a five minute stroll along Rochdale Road into Denshaw.**

Denshaw is a major junction of trans-Pennine routes, as the Oldham-Halifax and Rochdale-Huddersfield roads intersect. To add to things, the A6052 Delph road also climbs to this point. Small wonder the central pub is called the *Junction*. **Cross straight over the main road, and after just a few yards on the Huddersfield road, turn left up a short-lived track opposite the Post office/shop. The old way proper bears left off it, rising a sunken, part-walled, overgrown course across open ground: such is its potential for moisture that it can be easier to follow the track towards the church, then bear left to rejoin the way. It then rises an enclosed course to a gate into a farmyard.**

Bear across to the left, briefly, and from a gate rise left to another gate. Turn sharp right over a stile and away along the field top. From the next stile advance to the wall corner, then keep straight on across the sloping field centre, slanting gently down to the far corner. New Year's Bridge Reservoir appears ahead, backed by moorland. From here a faint old way slants down to a stile/gate back onto the A640.

Cross the road and go left just 80 yards, then turn right along the grassy dam of the reservoir. Here the uppermost reaches of the river Tame are crossed. **At the end go left with the wall as far as a stile/gate in it, to enter rough moorland. The path slants away left, charting a clear course to rise gently away through reedy surrounds, maintaining a straight line up to a dip in the skyline ahead. An iron ladder-stile admits onto a junction of old tracks.** This is a major meeting place of ways historic and modern, with the Oldham Way and Horseshoe Trail passing a home-made memorial guidepost. Here also the view south bursts onto the scene, to the hills and folds of Saddleworth, the higher ground including Pots & Pans and the Alphin ridge.

While the simplest way is to take the enclosed track (Broad Lane) rising to the right over Ox Hey Top, a better alternative awaits. **Briefly descend the firm trackway (Low Gate Lane) in front, and quickly take a gate in the sturdy wall on the right. Drop a little to the scant ruins below, then turn right along the crumbled old wallside.** Below, the two Castleshaw Reservoirs form a foreground to Millstone Edge and the high Pennine skyline. **At an old stile in a crumbled descending wall keep straight on, tracing sheeptrods that assist progress on this pleasant moor grass.**

As several faint descending walls are crossed, remember not to gain height but if anything lose the odd foot. Ultimately a stile is reached in a descending fence, and across rougher grass a distinctive sunken way is reached just beyond. Bear right up this, rising to a corner with a junction with Broad Lane at the house just above. This upper section can be short-cut by bearing left through a gateway at the bend, and tracing a thin path slanting left up the fieldside to join the now surfaced Broad Lane at a junction.

Bear left down the ridgetop road to the hamlet of Heights, with it church prominent. Beyond it across the upper Tame valley are the Bishop Park monument and Grains Bar. The hilltop settlement of Heights consists largely of the *Royal Oak*, a smashing old pub which could be any other cottage if its sign were to disappear overnight. The church of St. Thomas (Heights Chapel) served the community of Friarmere, an old name that still sees active service at the cricket club just down the hill. The church does not however, being closed and preserved by the Churches Conservation Trust.

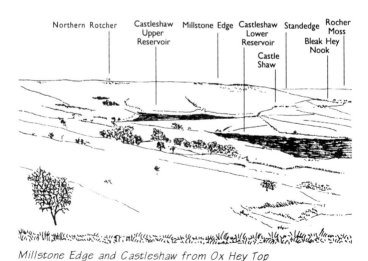

Millstone Edge and Castleshaw from Ox Hey Top

Leave the road by a stile, sharp right along the field top outside the churchyard. Before the end a green track slants down to a stile onto a narrow back road. Go left a few yards and turn down the nearside of a house. From the stile below, descend the fieldside until the wall turns away right, then continue down to a stile at the bottom. Cross a larger field aiming for the cricket pitch, and a gap-stile in the wall admits to its right side. Follow the drive out onto another road. Go left a couple of yards and turn down the nearside of a terraced row, continuing down a fieldside onto the A6052 Delph-Denshaw road.

Cross straight over and down a driveway through trees. At the bottom, just before it ends, turn left into a courtyard in a cluster of dwellings, and at the other side a cart track runs down a wooded bank. A continuing path runs on to a bridge on the infant River Tame. Across, turn downstream on a broad pathway, soon re-crossing the young river. The path runs down to the returning stream which leads a lovely few minutes' course down to the next footbridge.

On crossing, a thin path winds up the bank into a field. Rise straight up by a tiny stream, to a stile into the foot of gardens. Follow the drive up between the two houses, slanting up to Tamecroft Farm. On reaching the first barn, don't enter the yard, but rise to a stile on the left. Slant up to a small outbuilding, passing it and passing above the house, then climb the steep field, a few old stone steps leading to a stile onto the drive above. Look back up the valley to see Denshaw huddled around its church tower, the Windy Hill mast on the skyline behind, and Blackstone Edge looking shapely to the left.

The drive leads up onto the B6197 Grains Road. Go right and within 50 yards a path doubles back left up a sunken way through heathery moorland above a plantation. At the top it runs on to a junction of back roads. Turn right along Ship Lane, briefly, then take a path rising to the waiting monument crowning Bishop Park (see page 3). Not surprisingly this proves a superb vantage point, the vast sprawl of greater Manchester to the west, and the settled Pennine scene to the east. The monument records the gift of this land in 1927 to the people of Oldham in memory of William and Anne Bishop. An Ordnance Survey column stands to its south at 1230ft/375m. To finish head north over open ground, on a path down to a car park. Back on Ship Lane, follow this or the pitch & putt course for the few minutes back to Grains Bar. The road rejoins Grains Road on entering, and a bridleway cuts the corner on the near side of the *Kings Arms*.

6

CASTLESHAW FORT & MILLSTONE EDGE

START *Castleshaw*　　　　*Grid ref. SD 996090*

DISTANCE *6½ miles*

ORDNANCE SURVEY MAPS
1:50,000
Landranger 109 - Manchester
Landranger 110 - Sheffield & Huddersfield
1:25,000
Outdoor Leisure 1 - Peak District, Dark Peak
Outdoor Leisure 21 - South Pennines

ACCESS *Start from the public car park by the Castleshaw Centre, Waterworks Road, off the A62 Huddersfield Road east of Delph (top of Delph Lane). The main road is served by Oldham-Huddersfield buses. Alternative starts are Standedge (Brun Clough Reservoir car park on the top of the A62, SE 018094); and Diggle, both on the route.*

The impressive site of a Roman fort is a prelude to a splendid moorland tramp, concluding with the colourful country around Diggle.

S At the very outset the car park boasts views to the skyline cirque of Northern Rotcher and Millstone Edge. **At the far end of the car park a stile points the way across a field corner to join a back road. Turn left and down for a minute to a dip, where a path on the right is signed to the Roman fort. Climb diagonally up the field to a stile at the top accessing the site.** Castleshaw Roman fort was opened to the public in 1989 after excavation and conservation work. Though principally a military base guarding a road over the Pennines, it also served as the focal point of local life. Whilst appreciable work went into it, the site was only occupied for two fairly short periods, in the latter part of the 1st century and the start of the following one: this latter spell featured a smaller fort within the original's boundaries. When highlighted by a low sun the distinct grassy banks cast an evocative shadow over this impressive setting beneath the moors.

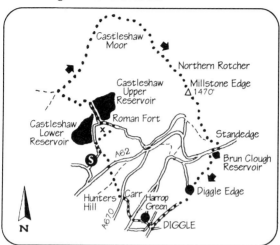

Resume with the fence on the right to the far end of the site, and on to a stile onto a lane in front of a house. Turn left down Dirty Lane, with Castleshaw Upper Reservoir in front. At a junction bear right on the embankment road, Castleshaw Top Bank. Around the head of the reservoir moorland slopes rise to the skyline of Northern Rotcher and Millstone Edge: indeed, most of our route is effectively highlighted (see also the illustration on page 28). **At the end turn left on the rough road to Wood Farm. Without entering, turn sharp right up an enclosed rough road, which rises quite steeply as Low Gate Lane, to gain the ridge at a multiple junction of unsurfaced walled ways.** New views to the north look over Rochdale to distant moorlands.

Turn sharp right here on Moor Lane, the way soon emerging to rise by a right-hand wall, a part sunken way over the knoll of Broadhead Noddle. Down to the left are the three contiguous reservoirs of the upper Tame valley. Our route also passes several Oldham Corporation Water Works stones. **The way becomes briefly enclosed again on the top to run to a gate/stile onto Castleshaw Moor. On the skyline ahead stands a prominent cairn, and the broad path ultimately winds up to gain it: now we're really on the tops.**

The path then bears right to run along the clear if featureless **edge,** **confirmed by occasional waymarks and cairns. A well-defined** **clough is crossed, and approaching an area of scattered rocks the** **going improves. At the start of the gritstone edge of Northern** **Rotcher, a stone marker post signals our merging with the Pennine** **Way. A splendid stride now heads along the crest of the scarp,** **looking down over the two Castleshaw reservoirs and much else.**

When the rocks abate the path runs on to approach the shorter-lived **grouping at Millstone Edge.** This earns new views to the east, overlooking the watershed to nearby Pule Hill backed by further moorland, and beyond that to Emley Moor TV mast. **The route passes** **the flat-topped Dinner Stone to arrive at the concrete Ordnance** **Survey column, at 1470ft/448m the summit of the walk.** This is very much a stage to savour as the weathered rock formations look down on Diggle and southwards to the hills above Saddleworth. Just before it, identified by a cairn above is a memorial stone recalling Ammon Wrigley, local poet and Saddleworth expert.

Resuming, the path drops gently down to a wall-stile off the moor **proper, and down through several stiles in old walls amid rough** **pastures. The last one returns us to moorland, with Brun Clough** **Reservoir and its car park on Standedge just below. The path drops** **down to join a firm track, which leads left out onto the A62** **Huddersfield-Oldham road.** Here we forsake the Pennine Way, but the Oldham Way and the Standedge Trail remain with us. The *Floating Light* pub is just two minutes west along the road. The Peak District National Park is here entered for little more than half a mile.

Cross to the car park at Brun Clough Reservoir, and turn right along **the roadside edge of the reservoir.** This small dam was one of many that were built to supply the Huddersfield Narrow Canal. **At the end** **turn left to a bridle-gate, from where a path drops down rough slopes** **to meet a cart track. Bear left on this, dropping down to a derelict** **house.** To the right is a circular airshaft dug for ventilation for the tunnel below.

Just past the house leave the track on a path dropping down to the **right. This shadows a wall down the moor edge outside and past large** **spoil heaps from the tunnel construction.** Over to the left a broad unfrequented side valley drives deep into the Pennines, containing the tiny Diggle Reservoir: Ravenstone Rocks feature on the skyline above. **A pleasant descent leads down to an access road by a house at Diggle Edge. Turn down the drive past the house, and this enclosed bridleway leads a steady course down into the top edge of Diggle.** This is Boat Lane, the route by which the canal ponies were led over the top of Standedge while the barges were 'legged' through the three-mile canal tunnel below (see page 79). **The lane emerges fortuitously alongside the imposing, three-storeyed *Diggle Hotel*, a welcome haven after a spell on the tops.**

Turn right at the road and over the railway. Immediately to the right is the tunnel entrance, with the smaller original tunnel to its right (again, see page 79 for more on the rail tunnels). **At the bridge end turn right, briefly, on Harrop Court Road, then sharp left up an enclosed footway in front of Ainsbrook Terrace. This emerges onto a narrow back road, go right the few yards to emerge onto Harrop Green.** This is a lovely spot, the attractive grouping of dwellings across a tree-shrouded green being a fine example of an old weaving settlement.

Bear left along Harrop Green Lane, passing further attractive groupings as the road descends to a crossroads with a broader road. To the left, ahead, modern 'Legoland' housing impinges greatly on the relative grandeur of Harrop Edge, above. **Cross straight over and down the very narrow and virtually traffic-free Carr Lane, which quickly turns to rise away. At a bend it begins a steep climb past the scattered dwellings at Carr and up onto the A670 road out of Saddleworth.**

Just a few yards to the right across the road, a rough track rises away, almost at once swinging right to slant gently up above some colourful mixed vegetation. This makes a grand foreground to views back over the valley to Standedge and the moorland skyline. **This firm old track rises through a minor nick in the skyline. Quickly reaching a crossroads on Hunters Hill, go straight over and down the rougher one.** Woodland on the right has not yet found its way onto the map. Directly in front now is Castleshaw Lower Reservoir.

The A62 is rejoined at the bottom, with the *Saddleworth Hotel* just along to the right. Cross over and down a short-lived driveway, Water's Gate. Passing right of the house, the old sunken way of Cote Lane descends between retaining walls to rejoin the access road that was left at the start.

DIGGLE

START *Uppermill*   *Grid ref. SD 996056*

DISTANCE *5 miles*

ORDNANCE SURVEY MAPS
1:50,000
Landranger 109 - Manchester
Landranger 110 - Sheffield & Huddersfield
1:25,000
Outdoor Leisure 1 - Peak District, Dark Peak

ACCESS *Start from the centre of Uppermill. Several small car parks. Served by bus from Manchester, Oldham, Ashton-under-Lyne and Huddersfield. Rail station a good half-mile distant at Greenfield.*

A straightforward ramble with only a tiny amount of early climbing. Glorious views over the Saddleworth area and a wealth of interest.

⑤ For a note on Uppermill see page 38. **Leave the main street south of the church, by the narrow Moorgate Street just before the Roman Catholic church of the Sacred Heart & St. William. This leads to a bridge over the Huddersfield Narrow Canal. Join the towpath and turn right, a short but absorbing stroll as far as the Brownhill Countryside Centre.** For more on the canal, see page 79.

En route we pass two locks, the second with a mighty railway viaduct above and the river Tame below. The 23-arch Saddleworth Viaduct carries the railway high above the river and canal just a mile and a half after it emerges from the gloom of Standedge Tunnel; the aqueduct is known as Old Sag due to a dip in its arch. Lime Kiln Lock was one of the first two locks to be restored in the early days of the canal's ambitious restoration. The Brownhill centre is based in a former council stables of 1916, and has displays and a shop.

At the front, cross the A670 with great care and head straight up the steep Brownhill Lane beneath the end of the viaduct. When it bends sharp left continue straight up a driveway. Note on the right here the impressive Lower Brownhill with its mullioned windows with tiny lights. The monument on Pots & Pans reveals itself over to the right. **When the drive swings left uphill again, go straight ahead on a level, tightly enclosed footway to emerge onto a private road.** Just ahead, it crosses a pathway on the line of the old Stalybridge-Diggle railway.

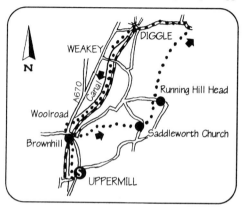

Just ahead the road forks: advance along the right branch which runs on as a fieldside track. Glorious views across the fields look to the moorland backdrop of Pots & Pans, with Saddleworth church tower standing proud up ahead. **Into the next field an old stile sees the now thinner path become briefly enclosed. From a stile at the end bear right, escaping poor drainage to another stile at a path junction. The improving path runs on into a small wooded clough. Climbing away up the other side the path splits above a delightful pond. Either way will lead up onto the back road by Saddleworth church, the left one being a little nicer. Turn right to the front of the church.**

Here is the bonus of the *Church Inn*, currently brewing its own wide range of beers. St. Chad's is a gaunt Victorian church high above the Saddleworth settlements, and outside is a set of stocks dated 1698. If wanting to create a quality pub crawl, it might be worth knowing that a second splendid pub is just two minutes distant: the *Cross Keys* with its marvellous interior can be found by a path slanting up the field in front of the church.

Turn up an enclosed path by the front of the church, up into the yard of the stables at Ivy Bank Farm. Rise straight up past the house and buildings, and as the drive swings right up to a road, instead go left to a stile by a gate. An enclosed grassy path heads away to cross a tiny clough. Advance straight on the fields, this fading, embanked old path leading on beneath the house at Wickens Farm. Beyond it the old path is picked up to enter another small wooded clough. Across the right branch, go straight on up above a deep-cut dry groove on the left. At the end bear right through a gateway to a ladder-stile onto the back road at Running Hill Head.

Almost opposite, a narrow snicket squeezes between the gardens of this attractive hamlet, emerging into a field. Big open views greet the eye, looking over the hillside above Diggle, with Millstone Edge on the skyline ahead and the brow of Ravenstone Rocks taking shape just over to the right. The generally straight path now follows the Peak National Park boundary. Enclosed as far as a stile, the path then crosses to the corner just ahead, where a clever recess hides a kissing-gate. Follow the right-hand wall down to a corner gate to resume on the other side of the wall, and at the bottom a green lane leading from the farm at Back o' th' Lee is met.

Across the green lane continue down through the next gateway, then bear left to a stile near the corner. As in several cases hereabouts, the traditional gap-stile has been consolidated with a modern step-stile. From the two slabs on a tiny stream behind, bear right across the scant remains of a wall to drop down to a single-slab bridge on a water channel. Bear right with it, a tractor track forming to lead out alongside it to a back road. Turning left this quiet road leads within ten minutes or so down into Diggle.

This upper part of Diggle is known as Diglea, whose fine grouping of cottages form the heart of an early weaving settlement. At the road end awaits the *Diggle Hotel*, a splendid pub at the foot of Boat Lane, the route by which the canal ponies were led over the top of Standedge while the boats were 'legged' through the three-mile canal tunnel. At the junction beneath the pub take the road over the railway. On the right is the tunnel entrance, with the smaller original tunnel to its right. At the bridge end go left on Station Road. Just after the bend turn into Diggle Fields car park on the left, at the end of which a path joins the canal towpath at the southern entrance to the Standedge Tunnel. After restoration work during 1999 this will once again be open.

The return route is now infallible as it simply follows the canal back, the last stage being a retracing of outward steps from Brownhill to Uppermill. There is much of interest en route, however, commencing at the first lock. This marks the start of the Diggle Flight, a major series of locks that were the last to be built on the canal. While the waterway was serviceable to Woolroad from 1799 (see below), this final stage, with all the work the locks entailed, was saved until the tunnel itself was near completion.

By the time a road bridge at Weakey is reached there is the option of paths on either bank, as the Diggle Flight leads delightfully down to the A670 at Woolroad. The final section was still missing in 1999, though a navigable culvert will be in place by the time the canal is fully operational in 2001 (the path reverts to the left side only for the final yards to the main road). Just along to the right is the suitably named *Navigation* pub. **Across the road the route encounters the canalside Wool Road Transhipment Warehouse.** This was built 200 years ago when the Standedge Tunnel was under construction, to deal with the loading of goods on and off the narrowboats for carriage over Standedge to Marsden. After various uses it has miraculously survived to this day, now restored to former glories as part of the canal's renaissance. **The towpath then leads on to a narrow section beneath the A6052 Delph road and back to Brownhill.**

Saddleworth Viaduct and the Huddersfield Narrow Canal

8

DOBCROSS & DELPH

START *Uppermill*   *Grid ref. SD 996056*

DISTANCE *5½ miles*

ORDNANCE SURVEY MAPS
1:50,000
Landranger 109 - Manchester
1:25,000
Outdoor Leisure 1 - Peak District, Dark Peak

ACCESS *Start from the centre of Uppermill. Several small car parks. Served by bus from Manchester, Oldham, Ashton-under-Lyne and Huddersfield. Rail station a good half-mile distant at Greenfield.*

An absorbing walk taking in two of Saddleworth's classic villages.

S Uppermill is the principal settlement of Saddleworth, a loose-knit collection of villages spread around the headwaters of the river Tame. Saddleworth is the name of an ancient parish, and its absence from the map can confuse first-time visitors. As its name suggests, Uppermill owed its growth to the advent of textile mills. Today Saddleworth is fashionable, and Uppermill has a museum featuring working textile machinery among its exhibits, a craft centre, shops, cafes and pubs. A major attraction is the Huddersfield Narrow Canal (see page 79).

Leave the main street south of the church, by narrow Moorgate Street just before the Roman Catholic church. This leads to a canal bridge where the walk will conclude. For now cross the bridge and just ahead turn left up an enclosed path. This rises through colourful surrounds to cross the railway line, and continues up to a path junction. Back to the left are fine views over Uppermill to Pots & Pans and round to the Saddleworth edges on the sprawling flanks of Black Hill. **Turn left at the path junction to rise onto a narrow back road.**

Cross straight over and up a slim path through heather, with the old Moorgate Quarry hidden on the left. The appearance of a golf club comes as a sudden surprise on the right, as the path continues up to a stile onto more open surrounds. Over to the left is the tall TV mast on Wharmton. **Advance a few yards to a grassy track junction and turn right to a wall-stile just above. Here stands a golfers' rest hut.** The environs of the 14th tee are a good place to take stock, looking back to the Chew Valley, featuring Alphin Pike, Dove Stones Reservoir beneath Dove Stone Rocks, Pots & Pans, up beyond to the Pennine skyline crossing Black Hill and Saddleworth Moor.

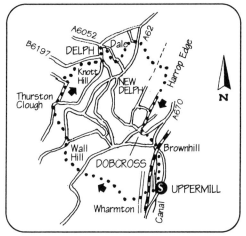

Head directly away across the course, on a clear track that soon improves in nature and bears the grand title of Colt Hill Lane. Big views ahead and to the right feature Millstone Edge and Standedge as part of a long watershed skyline. **When the track finally fades on our last fairway, advance on to a pair of forlorn stone gateposts ahead, and a contrastingly thin path runs on to a wall-stile beyond. Cross the field to a stile/gate onto Burnedge Lane.**

Go left just 75 yards to a gate on the right. Descend with the wallside to a factory secreted at the bottom. A track swings left in front of it to enter its car park, and its access road climbs steeply to a road junction at Wall Hill. Turn right along the upper road, the A62. On the opposite side, after the heathery bank ends, take a gate on the left from where a firm track rises away. It leads to a stile into the grounds of the lone house (Greaves) in front, from where pass the house and follow its drive up onto Thurston Clough Road. Prominent up ahead is a concentration of crumbled field walls.

Turn right to descend to the clough itself, and as the road runs back out, turn sharp left up a narrow, steep back road. This levels out to run on to a T-junction with Knott Hill Lane. Go left briefly, then take a gap-stile in the wall on the right just before the first house. Cross to a wall corner just ahead, then go sharp right away from the house onto a well defined ridge. This presents new views north, down over the modern part of Delph backed by Castleshaw Upper Reservoir and its Pennine watershed skyline. From the corner stile descend the side of the pasture alongside a reedy sunken way. As it swings right, away from the wall it becomes more amenable, to slant down the steep pasture towards Delph. It runs on above a fence to a stile at the end, then as an enclosed green way above rows of houses. A house on the left at the end bears a 1740 datestone. Passing through a cluster of houses it drops down as an access road into the village centre.

Once a bustling little mill community, Delph now enjoys more peaceful times as an integral player in the now fashionable Saddleworth scene. Opened in 1851 and closed just over a century later was Delph's own tiny branch railway. Popularly referred to as the Delph Donkey Line, it was originally a horse-drawn affair. Turn left (Stoneswood Road) onto King Street, noting the library at the junction. Dating from 1899 it sports a fine clock tower high above its converging sheltered front. Head along the street past several pubs and shops, and a chippy with a 1769 datestone. The impressive three-storeyed *Swan Inn* on the left is a former coaching inn. Across the bridge on the river Tame are toilets and the attractive and historic *White Lion*, featuring some mullioned windows.

Without crossing the bridge, turn right along Bridge End, and a track runs downstream with the river and a mill-race to Shore Mill just ahead. Now a private house, this splendid three-storeyed building dates back over two hundred years, and the race that once served a waterwheel has also been splendidly restored. Continuing past it the race returns to lead straight on past a footbridge and the car park. Look up across the car park to see the self-explanatory *Union is Strength - Co-operative Hall 1864* on a building opposite. Cross a metal footbridge at the end to resume downstream on a broader track through trees opposite the big stone-built Valley Mill, also known as Rasping Mill. Emerging into the yard of the large red-brick Lumb Mill, double back sharply left up a footway through trees onto Hill End Road (a flight of steps short-cuts the upper section).

Turn right on the road, and after the cluster of houses where it becomes Rumbles Lane, go left along the access road of Dale Fields. Towards the end of the red-brick houses, the path shuffles right to resume as an enclosed way through the fields. Quickly entering the cluster at Dale turn right on the access road out onto Sandbed Lane. Bear right up this onto the A62 Oldham-Huddersfield road.

Opposite, just a few yards to the left, a stile sends a path slanting right, up to another stile in the descending fence. The path continues up through pleasant pastures, keeping right at a junction to fade at the grassy hummocks of a small quarry site. Continue slanting up to a guidepost and along to the far corner of the field, where a stile admits onto the rough surfaced Harrop Edge Lane. Cross straight over and head away along the wallside, over the brow to emerge at another stile just above Harrop Edge. Advance to the edge and turn right. Harrop Edge offers a bird's-eye view down steep, rough vegetated slopes to the environs of Diggle, featuring the parallel canal and railway, and a massive timber works. It goes without saying that the usual culprits such as Standedge and Pots & Pans are in evidence.

The Square, Dobcross

41

The smashing path runs on to a junction of walled byways. Go straight ahead on the main one (Long Lane) dropping gently as Platt Hill Lane comes in on the right to become surfaced at a fine row of houses. The lane offers a good view ahead to the Saddleworth Viaduct. **Continue straight down to merge into Sandy Lane on the edge of Dobcross. Bear right past the Congregational Chapel and into The Square.**

The heart of this old village oozes character, with some splendid houses stood around. Two centuries ago Dobcross was more influential to the Saddleworth area than Uppermill, and a number of former weavers' cottages pre-date the arrival of the larger mills in the valleys. The centrepiece of the Square includes, appropriately, a splendid pub the *Swan*, which epitomises just what a real pub should be like. Also in evidence are a 1900 memorial to WHF Ramsden, surgeon and physician, and the old Saddleworth Bank.

Turn left at the Square, the road becoming Sugar Lane. As it bends left go straight ahead down Nicker Brow. On the right stands the substantial Bridge House, birthplace of Henry Platt in 1793. He was a founder of Platt Brothers of Oldham, who became the world's largest manufacturers of textile machinery. **After a cluster of cottages the brow becomes an urban footway, which descends to more houses at a bridge on the Tame.** The remarkable three-storeyed house on the left features mullioned windows and shows ample evidence of an earlier period as a mill. Note also the stone arched bridge on the river, long since made redundant by the 'modern' bridge.

Cross the bridge to the main junction (A6502/A670) and go right into the grounds of Brownhill Countryside Centre. Based in a former council stables of 1916, this visitor centre features interesting displays and includes a shop. **Join the canal towpath and go left to conclude the walk by returning to the next bridge at Uppermill.** At the start is a remarkable array of features as we pass a lock, under a mighty railway viaduct and at the same time bridge the river Tame on an aqueduct. The Saddleworth Viaduct of 1849 (illustrated on page 37) carries the railway high above the river and canal just a mile and a half after it emerges from the gloom of Standedge Tunnel. After another lock and some attractive wooded slopes opposite it is a steady and all too short amble back. Some sturdy stepping-stones on the river offer an alternative finish directly into the centrally sited public park.

POTS & PANS

START Binn Green   Grid ref. SE 016044

DISTANCE 4½ miles

ORDNANCE SURVEY MAPS
1:50,000
Landranger 110 - Sheffield & Huddersfield
1:25,000
Outdoor Leisure 1 - Peak District, Dark Peak

ACCESS Start from the Binn Green car park on the A635 Holmfirth Road a mile east of the edge of Greenfield. Greenfield is served by bus from Oldham.

A superb walk on grand paths to a fine little hill. A perfect introduction to the area.

❺ Though Alderman's Hill looms over the car park to the north, its finest prospect is across to the Dove Stone edges. **From the car park return to the road and cross to a broad, rough track heading off to the left. This is Long Lane, and soon settles down to a nice green course between walls, with Alderman's Hill high above.** Striding along there are good views down over Dove Stone Reservoir backed by Chew Brook and the Alphin ridge, and ahead across Greenfield to Wharmton; on rounding a corner the Pots & Pans monument appears on the skyline above. **Ignoring lesser tracks at a junction keep straight on, the way improving into a superb old footway. Across a tiny clough the way rises out into more open terrain, and on the brow swings right as a broader track onto a road at Knowl Top Farm.**

At this point an inviting grassy old way makes a shorter route up onto Pots & Pans, though our more rewarding option devotes much more time to the open moor. **Advance along the road, Knowl Top Lane, as**

far as the drive to Knowl Farm on the left. En route we pass an impressive three-storeyed house with mullioned windows set back to the left. **Leave the road by a drive on the right, a fine flagged effort which rises to approach a lone house. Don't follow it down but take a stile in front, and a faint path runs on above the garden.** Far below, the Saddleworth scene is centred around the massive railway viaduct. **The gurgling White Brook Spring is passed and the way runs a level course, with Saddleworth church tower appearing ahead. The path is a real gem as it traverses increasingly colourful moor-like terrain to approach Pobgreen, ultimately becoming enclosed by old walls.**

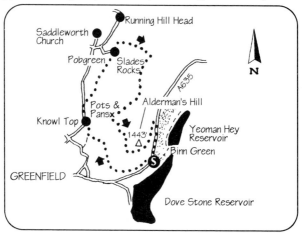

Pobgreen is a classic hillside hamlet with mullioned windows aplenty, from the first cottages to a stunning three-storeyed former weaver's house. **The access road is joined just beneath the big house.** If seeking refreshment then an excellent pub is just two minutes away: follow the lane down onto the road to find the near-hidden *Cross Keys*. **The main route turns just a few yards up the rough road in the hamlet, then heads off along a gently rising grassy lane on the left. At a sharp bend it climbs towards the base of the steeper slopes.** Over to the left is the ruined farmhouse of Slades Barn, clearly once of some character, while to the right is a sorry picture of crumbling field walls. **On open pastures the track fades, but advance straight on to the steeper slopes where sunken pathways climb to the edge of the moorland plateau.** By now there are panoramic views back over Saddleworth to Wharmton, Dobcross, Harrop Edge and round to Millstone Edge.

The path turns right along the moor edge, alongside a crumbled wall above the appreciable tumble of Slades Rocks. To the south-east, the skyline from Holme Moss to Alphin overtops our more modest height. Ahead and a little lower, our objective of the Pots & Pans monument appears. **As the wall drops away the path runs over the moor to the tilted outcrops of Shaw Rocks. Here the path forks, though both join a broad cross-path just two minutes ahead: the thinner left branch passes the rounded Sugar Loaf rock. Joining the broad path turn right, and it slants down to a saddle before a short rise through an old wall to the war memorial on Pots & Pans. Just up to the right before it, the shapely assortment of Kinder Stones tempt a detour.**

Partly enclosed by iron railings this sturdy monument was erected by Saddleworth folk to commemorate their dead of the Great War, with inevitable sad additions a quarter of a century later. Its prominent position overlooking the green and pleasant homeland of those who made the ultimate sacrifice will bring a lump to the throat of anyone with a hint of human emotion. Alderman's Hill brings this spur of moorland to a shapely culmination over to the left.

Leave by a grassy path heading south the few yards to the characterful Pots & Pan Stone. A scramble to the top reveals deep circular bowls weathered by the forces of nature on this windswept spot. **Beneath it a green path slants down to the left, past an old quarry and down to a path crossroads by a wall at Edge End. Turn left to rise gently away with the wall. The faint path maintains this same course as it curves round the upper flank of Alderman's Hill. Swinging round beneath the brow some splendid rockscapes are revealed just above, competing for our attention with a grand prospect across to the Dove Stone edges rising formidably above Dove Stone Reservoir.**

When the wall turns sharply away ignore an unofficial path descending to Long Lane, just below. The true path heads straight on (not one slanting slightly down), a faint, dead-level trod. Ahead, Yeoman Hey and Greenfield reservoirs enter the scene. **The thin trod leads unfailingly on beneath the rocks, reaching a few boulders at a steeper drop to a bouldery hollow. The path remains clear as it curves round and gently down beneath the last of the rocks, our goal being a roadside phone box just above Yeoman Hey Plantation. A lively spring is passed as the thin trod slants across to a stile onto the road opposite the phone box. Cross to the footway which doubles back down outside the trees to quickly return to the car park.**

10

GREENFIELD

START Dove Stone Reservoir   Grid ref. SE 013034

DISTANCE 6½ miles

ORDNANCE SURVEY MAPS
1:50,000
Landranger 109 - Manchester
Landranger 110 - Sheffield & Huddersfield
1:25,000
Outdoor Leisure 1 - Peak District, Dark Peak

ACCESS Start from the Dove Stone Reservoir car park, on Bank Lane off the A635 Holmfirth Road, a mile east of Greenfield. An alternative start is Greenfield railway station, just off the route mid-walk. Greenfield is served by bus from Oldham and Manchester.

Easy walking in a typical mix of urban and rural surrounds.

⑤ **From the toilet block and information boards turn away from the reservoir along Bradbury's Lane. Passing a nice three-storeyed house with mullions down on the right, the road quickly expires at a long terraced row.** The 'corporate' paintwork identifies this as a row of millworkers' cottages. **At the very end of the terrace and road, take an urban path slanting down between the fields. At the bottom it drops to a path junction just before Greenfield Brook.**

Without advancing to the footbridge turn left, and the path runs briefly enclosed to emerge over a water leat and into better surroundings downstream with the brook. Absorbing a works drive it runs on to a bridge onto a road. Go left to the main junction just ahead, and keep left at the *Clarence Hotel* **along the A635 Holmfirth Road. Cross over, and after bridging the beck and ignoring a first footpath down to a footbridge, go a little further to a second one.**

The path descends through new housing to rejoin the brook down to a stone arched road bridge. Cross and turn left on Greenbridge Lane. Merging into the main road keep left, passing a Post office and the *Wellington* pub. Just short of the main junction at the end, drop left onto the towpath of the Huddersfield Narrow Canal. This is not to be confused with the river Tame, which is crossed immediately beforehand. •For the railway station start, drop down the Chew Valley Road past the *Railway* pub to a junction, and along it just a few yards over the canal bridge to then turn right down onto the towpath.

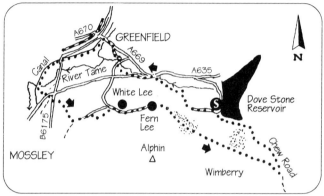

So begins a grand stroll along the towpath. For more on the canal see page 79. Opposite are some three-storeyed former weavers' houses. Neglected sections of canal will shortly see restoration, though some parts reclaimed by nature will probably lose a little of their charm. Views left look to the moorland ridge of Alphin on the south side of the Chew Valley. **Another nice corner is reached at a lock alongside Royal George Mills, which date back over 200 years.** Alongside are attractive cottages, while the lock's narrowness explains the canal's title. **Across the road bridge the towpath advances to another lock, then an aqueduct carries us over the Tame on two low stone arches.**

Just beyond, at the next bridge, leave the towpath and turn up onto the rough road above. Follow this left up onto the A635, with the *Royal George* pub just along to the left. Cross straight over and up the short-lived Shadows Lane, becoming a footpath as it crosses a track and up via tiny Shadworth Close onto the B6175 Greenfield-Mossley road. The trackway exploits the old course of the Stalybridge-Diggle railway, parallel with the surviving one across the river.

Cross straight over the 'B' road, noting the old boundary stone at the start of the steep Shadworth Lane. Climb the rough lane, which at the top becomes a more engaging footway to emerge into more open surrounds. Views north open out to survey the Saddleworth scene backed by rolling moors. Continue up, becoming a broader track to rise onto Moor Edge Road. Go left along this rough road, which acquires a surface as it starts to descend. Opposite a fine house take a stile on the right from were a very clear path contours across the heather-clad moorland beneath Alphin Pike.

The main path curves in to cross a small clough by way of stone slabs, then contours back out and past a ruin to a stile back onto a corner of heather moorland. This time take the track down the near side to descend onto Intake Lane. Opposite stands aptly named White Lee, with it three storeys and mullioned windows. Turn right along this narrow access road, which runs a pleasant course beneath the moorland slopes of Alphin Brow. The road terminates at a cluster of fine stone houses (Fern Lee Farm), with a fork just beyond. The left branch is Bradbury's Lane, which makes for a direct return. At this point we enter the Peak National Park for the remainder of the walk.

The full route bears right on Intake Lane, a grand old way between crumbled walls. It slants gently up to run on through a sizeable plantation, emerging above the farm of Kinder Intake. The start point is below, with Dove Stone Reservoir much more prominent under the Dove Stone edges. The way runs more faintly on across a large grassy pasture and a stream, to a kissing-gate in a wall into Chew Piece Plantation. This scattered oakwood is littered with numerous large boulders. A lovely stroll leads back out to a rougher scene directly beneath the bristly skyline of Wimberry, a popular climbing ground.

The old way runs unfailingly on through the jumble of Wimberry Stones. The track's permanence is due its origin as the course of the Chew Valley Tramway, used to transport clay to the Chew Reservoir site in 1914 (a journey of about four miles from the main line). The path curves round above Chew Brook to approach the deeper, wilder confines of its upper reaches. At a breached embankment the brook is crossed on a footbridge, after which the old way is left and a path clambers left up onto the Chew Road, access road for the reservoir visited in WALK 11. Turn left down this, a grand simple stride to finish. At the bottom it swings left past the boat enclosure and clubhouse of Dove Stone Sailing Club to return to the car park.

11

DOVE STONE ROCKS

START *Dove Stone Reservoir*   *Grid ref. SE 013034*

DISTANCE *5¼ miles*

ORDNANCE SURVEY MAPS
1:50,000
Landranger 110 - Sheffield & Huddersfield
1:25,000
Outdoor Leisure 1 - Peak District, Dark Peak

ACCESS *Start from Dove Stone Reservoir car park, on Bank Lane off the A635 a mile east of Greenfield. Greenfield is served by bus from Oldham and Manchester.* • *ACCESS AREA - see page 8.*

A classic moorland 'edge' walk high above a scenic reservoir.

S Dove Stone Reservoir was only completed in 1967, vastly enlarging the gathering capacity of the valley of Greenfield Brook, whose two smaller reservoirs are immediately upstream. **From the toilet block and information boards rise up the road to the corner of the dam just above, and head off along the top of its grassy embankment. At the end of the dam the path bends up to the shore, giving an immediate choice of paths. The upper one is used in WALK 12, so this time take the shoreline one. It offers glorious views across the water to appraise the walk in store, with the Dove Stone edges instilling eager anticipation. The track runs on to rise to an access road at the foot of Yeoman Hey Reservoir.** This was built in 1880 for Oldham's growing industrial demands. A stone proclaims it was laid by HM the King of Tonga in 1981, a century late for the official opening.

Take the rough road across the dam and turn right on it. However, just 20 yards after the sturdy wall on the left, turn up a faint yet distinct broad path, forging a bee-line up the steep grassy hillside. Up ahead is the craggy frown of Dove Stones. **On easing out on a brow with Dove Stone Clough in front, the path turns left to climb again on a broad spur, steeply for a while before curving more gently around to the right. With the rugged head of the clough in front, the path rises to a junction near the solitary Ashway Stone under the rim of the moor edge.** Looking back along the edge is Ashway Cross, visited on WALK 12 and easily incorporated into this excursion.

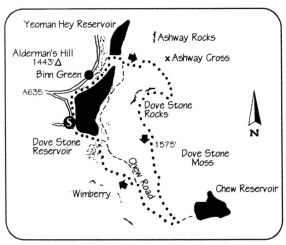

Turn right to approach upper Dove Stone Clough. Here there is a choice, of sorts, for a rising path past the stone runs on to encounter greater bare peat than an initially indistinct lower one: this runs on to a footbridge before slanting round to meet the higher way at the clough. Avoid the temptation of a short-cut into the head of the clough, for by running a little further 'inland' an easy natural ford leads effortlessly across. The old trod returns above Great Dovestone Rocks, soon reaching the hugely prominent memorial cairn on the Fox Stone.

The cairn recalls two local climbers who were killed in the Dolomites in 1972. This is a magnificent place for a break, overlooking a fine prospect of Dove Stone Reservoir, further illuminated when peppered with the colourful sails of boats. Note also Alderman's Hill rising behind Binn Green, with the monument on Pots & Pans now in view. Beneath the Dove Stone Rocks proper are some large quarried cliffs.

The edge route now heads due south, soon passing the ruin of the once substantial Bramley's Cot. The way leads past more splendid outcrops to Charnel Clough and along to the Dish Stone. Swinging round yet again the walk runs past the expiring rocky edge to an old quarry, cut to provide material for the dam of Chew Reservoir, just above. Turn down past it to gain the surfaced access road, and with the reservoir in such proximity it may be worth a stroll up to its corner. It was built in 1912, then the highest reservoir in the country.

The road offers a rapid descent and a direct return, with good views out from the enclosing walls of the upper Chew Valley. The big knoll of Stable Stones Brow increases in grandeur up to the left, with the climbing ground of Wimberry entering the scene beyond. At a boulder the road becomes unsurfaced, with Dove Stone Reservoir ahead. At a stile at Charnel Clough we leave Open Country, and the road becomes surfaced again. Although it leads unfailingly back, an optional finish awaits. Deviating left, a thin green path drops to a footbridge over Chew Brook, and onto a prominent embankment. This is the course of the Chew Valley Tramway, used to transport clay from Mossley for the construction of the Chew dam.

Continue until just before the scattered Chew Piece Plantation. The path in there is non-existent, so better to turn down before it to a huge boulder, continuing downstream with the brook on a good path past a weir, through trees and back onto the road. Turning left it runs along past the moored yachts and sailing clubhouse to return to the dam of Dove Stone Reservoir, and thus the car park.

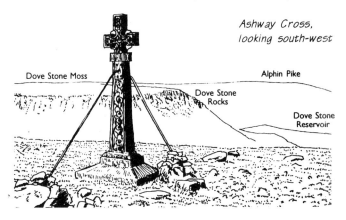

Ashway Cross, looking south-west

Dove Stone Moss

Alphin Pike

Dove Stone Rocks

Dove Stone Reservoir

12

BIRCHEN CLOUGH & RAVEN STONES

START *Dove Stone Reservoir*   *Grid ref. SE 013034*

DISTANCE *6 miles*

ORDNANCE SURVEY MAPS
1:50,000
Landranger 110 - Sheffield & Huddersfield
1:25,000
Outdoor Leisure 1 - Peak District, Dark Peak

ACCESS *Start from Dove Stone Reservoir car park, on Bank Lane off the A635 a mile east of Greenfield. Greenfield is served by bus from Oldham and Manchester. •ACCESS AREA - see page 8.*

A chain of attractive reservoirs set the scene for some spectacular rock scenery which includes a mini-scramble in Birchen Clough. The walk could be shortened by starting from Binn Green car park.

S Dove Stone Reservoir was completed in 1967, vastly enlarging the gathering capacity of the valley of Greenfield Brook, whose two smaller reservoirs will soon be encountered. **From the toilet block and information boards rise up the road to the corner of the dam just above, and head off along the top of its grassy embankment.** Crossing the dam, spare a glimpse to the factory below: another world maybe, but they didn't just settle here for the scenery, the acidic water coming off the moors is ideal for manufacturing fine paper. **At the end of the dam the path bends up to the shore, giving an immediate option of a simple shoreline path to the head of the reservoir. For greater interest take a stile just above, and a higher level path runs on above trees then into them. When it forks keep right for a level walk through a mix of woodland to rejoin the other path at a gate, where an access road comes down to the dam of Yeoman Hey Reservoir.**

A rough road runs alongside the reservoir below Yeoman Hey Plantation, but as it rises gently away, branch right on a grassy track remaining with the reservoir. It runs on past the reservoir head towards the grassy dam of Greenfield Reservoir, then just before it swings up left to the main access road (not as per map). Turn right to reach the dam of the third and final reservoir (built 1903). The surroundings have now grown in stature and austerity, with the dam dwarfed by the prow of Ashway Rocks. Past the reservoir head is Greenfield Brook, with the Raven Stones towering high above.

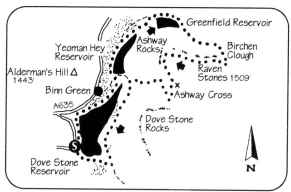

Yet again take the track along the reservoir side and into the rougher clough. Greenfield Brook is traced to its formation at the meeting of Holme and Birchen Cloughs. Throughout this the tumbling stream is a sheer delight, with an engaging fall over a series of ledges, and the Trinnacle on Raven Stones outstanding up above. At the confluence skirt around a tunnel entrance to embrace Birchen Clough, the right-hand ravine. The tunnel was made to convey excess water away in times of severe downpour on the moors: an old water board notice is a superfluous warning against exploration. To the left above Holme Clough, a fine jumble of boulders fall from beneath Lamb Knoll.

Birchen Clough offers a fine clamber up a bouldery ravine where the agile will make greater progress. The main path soon crosses to the opposite bank for most of the short climb. Above a minor scramble at some cascades, re-cross and double steadily back up the easier slopes on the right, an improving path running back to a promontory overlooking the confluence. Just before this is a new fence designed to exclude sheep in order to achieve regeneration of the vegetation.

A short distance further is the inspiring rock pinnacle suitably named the **Trinnacle.** Again, only the agile will contemplate the scramble it offers: the secret is to climb the easier second one, then for those with nerve it is a simple short stride onto its higher neighbour. **The clear edge path continues, a classic stride above gritstone outcrops looking down on Greenfield Reservoir. At a notable fork remain on the edge path.** The peatier moorland route runs past Major's Cairn (dedicated to a faithful dog), unseen from the edge path.

The main path holds to the edge to run above Ashway Rocks, and a splendid moment is revealed as their flat crest is topped, trading Greenfield Reservoir for a sweeping prospect of its two larger neighbours. Seen further along the edge, Dove Stone Rocks rise across the deep divide of Dove Stone Clough. Distantly is the sprawl of greater Manchester, contrasting sharply with the wild moors nearer to hand. A direct option here is to continue until the rocks fade, then angle straight down the grassy slope to pick up the descent path.

To visit Ashway Cross, bear left on the pathless moor for a very minor rise onto a stony edge revealing the cross just ahead. Ashway Cross (illustrated on page 51) is a memorial to James Platt, Member of Parliament for Oldham, who was the victim of a shooting accident here during a grouse shoot in 1857. **From the cross simply keep on the minor edge towards the rugged head of Dove Stone Clough. The improving path runs on towards the solitary Ashway Stone, but here be ready for the junction with a path climbing from the right.** The rapid descent starts here, though if wishing to remain high-level by taking in the Dove Stone edge, turn to WALK 11.

Double back down the slanting path which makes a splendid and very rapid return to the valley. Curving down the grassy flank it swings a little more steeply down to reveal a footbridge (not used) in the clough down to the left. The dark wall of Dove Stone Rocks remains as sombre as ever high to the left. **On gentler ground the path swings down to the right, commencing a faint yet distinct bee-line aiming for the rough road in front of the head of Dove Stone Reservoir, which it joins just short of the dam of Yeoman Hey Reservoir. Turn left on this to run south above plantations alongside Dove Stone Reservoir to lead to the Chew Road in the deep valley of Chew Brook. Turning right it crosses the brook to run past the moored yachts and sailing clubhouse to return to the dam of Dove Stone Reservoir.**

13

MARSDEN CLOUGH

START Digley   Grid ref. SE 110072

DISTANCE 6¼ miles

ORDNANCE SURVEY MAPS
1:50,000
Landranger 110 - Sheffield & Huddersfield
1:25,000
Outdoor Leisure 1 - Peak District, Dark Peak

ACCESS Start from the Yorkshire Water car park at the north side of Digley Reservoir, three-quarters of a mile off the A6024 at both Holme and Holmbridge. Both villages are also on the route, and are served by bus from Huddersfield via Holmfirth.

A memorable blend of attractive reservoirs, old lanes, fine moorland and colourful cloughs.

S Digley Reservoir is a relatively modern addition to the water catchment of the upper Holme Valley, having arrived on the scene in 1952. The car park has been created in a landscaped quarry which had provided stone for construction of the dam. **From the gate opposite the car park a path drops down the heathery bank above the reservoir to rejoin the road lower down.** At once there are grand views over the reservoir to the moorland slopes of Black Hill. **Continue the short way to a junction at the end of the dam. Don't cross the dam but continue down the road, soon reaching a kissing-gate on the right. The path runs briefly parallel with the road before slanting down through the trees, and from a corner kissing-gate it descends steps onto an access road, Digley Road. Turn left on this for a traffic-free walk into Holmbridge, the surface improving as the church tower appears in front, emerging past modern housing and the nicely sited cricket field.**

Holmbridge is based around the confluence of Marsden Clough with the river Holme. Centrepiece is St. David's imposing church, with the *Bridge Tavern* well placed. **Turn right over the bridge and go left on a side road signed to Yate Holme. When it splits take the right branch, Bank Lane.** Set into the wall on the left is a well, dated 1834. **The road becomes Brownhill Lane as it climbs past a restaurant to a junction. Keep straight on past several houses to reach the dam of Brownhill Reservoir, then continuing on to approach a road-end car park overlooking Ramsden Reservoir.** The section above the grounds of Brownhill Reservoir is a charming stroll with increasingly lovely views over its colourful banks to the Black Hill skyline. Approaching the Ramsden dam, Holme appears on the hill across, while there is also a grand view up the length of this upper reservoir.

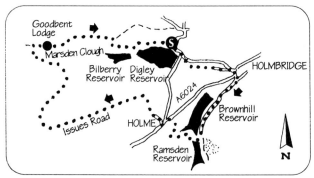

Just short of the car park an enclosed path turns down to cross the grassy dam of Ramsden Reservoir just below its crest. Downstream is the attractive head of Brownhill Reservoir. **At the end the path slants away from the dam, up through the trees onto a knoll on the spur between the two arms of Brownhill Reservoir. It then curves delightfully round above the wooded bank until dropping down to a footbridge on Rake Dike.** This feeder of Brownhill Reservoir's western arm boasts a lovely waterfall.

Slanting back up the other side the path levels out of the trees, then up a small rough pasture to adjacent stiles at the top corner above a wood. An enclosed path rises to a stile, then up the other side of the wall to a gate/stile. On the left is an architect's self-designed house almost entirely below ground level. **The enclosed path runs out onto the A6024 on the edge of Holme. Turn left as far as a cobbled square.**

En route we pass Holme Castle Country Hotel with its castellated block, and a former school, still complete with its bell and inscription *Holme School rebuilt by subscription 1838*; the date 1694 is carved on the door lintel. Holme is a small but historic settlement nestled beneath the infamous Woodhead Road climbing to Holme Moss. Its attractive cottages include some three-storeyed weavers' houses. The *Fleece Inn* is just a few yards further along the road.

Turn up the square and the no-through-road. Note a 1696 datestone on the arch at the small playground entrance. **The road rises past the school and loses its surface as it winds away. At a fork keep left, rising to a patch of open ground graced with a seat.** This enjoys a view of Digley Reservoir, with the Wessenden Head Moor skyline up ahead. **Keep left on the main track, which as Issues Road commences a long, very gradual rise onto Stopes Moor.** Ahead are the attractive brows of Issue Edge and Black Dike Head, where the Pennine Way escapes the peaty plateau of Black Hill. **On finally shrugging off the walls the track advances more happily onto the moor, quickly reaching a branch right.** This is our grassy footpath, though the temptation of Issue Clough with its newly revealed rock-walled waterfall is strong.

Bearing right, the branch path curves down with the remains of a wall, crossing the stream and heading away on a good firm footing. It runs along the heathery moor of Good Bent before curving down to steep-walled Marsden Clough. Across, Goodbent Lodge stands amid a sorry scene of crumbling field walls, while downstream the clough enters a ravine-like enclave. **The track slants down to a footbridge.** This appears superfluous given the decent ford alongside, but is nevertheless a grand spot alongside the charming confluence of Dean Clough and Reap Hill Clough. **The steep track zigzags left up the other bank then rises as a gentler grassy way to a gate. Continue up the old wall-side to a stile/gate onto Nether Lane, a walled track. Turn right down this, past Goodbent Lodge and the old farm of Bartin. Black Hill spreads its shoulders to the right, with Digley Reservoir ahead. The track runs on with increasing views over the reservoir.**

At a major junction take the branch down to the right, a similarly wide walled track which drops left to another such junction at a patch of open ground. Keeping left this runs on before becoming a footpath outside the trees enclosing Digley Reservoir. It rejoins a track at the point where the old sunken way runs forlornly into the engulfing waters. This rises past an old quarry and on to the car park.

UPPER HOLME VALLEY

START *Ramsden*   *Grid ref. SE 115056*

DISTANCE *5¼ miles*

ORDNANCE SURVEY MAPS
1:50,000
Landranger 110 - Sheffield & Huddersfield
1:25,000
Outdoor Leisure 1 - Peak District, Dark Peak

ACCESS *Start from Yorkshire Water's Ramsden Reservoir car park, three-quarters of a mile off the A6024 at Holmbridge. Holmbridge is an alternative start point on the route, with buses from Huddersfield.*

Easy walking and varied surroundings around the headwaters of the river Holme. This walk is within the Peak District National Park as far as the crossroads above Digley Reservoir.

❺ From the car park continue along the unsurfaced road, passing a lone house to reach and cross the dam of Riding Wood Reservoir. Its embankment gives glorious views over the waters and past the plantations to the forbidden spurs and folds of Ramsden Clough; downstream is Ramsden Reservoir. **The old road runs on between plantations. Beneath the grassy dam of Yateholme Reservoir, leave it by a path on the right. This descends a broad break in the trees to a gateway overlooking Netherley Clough.** This steep flanked valley presents a colourful scene, with Ramsden Reservoir downstream.

A broad path slants down to a footbridge, then sets about the same task on the other side. However, take an early branch climbing steeply left, which if missed, has another branch doubling back immediately before a small sidestream. The improving path eases out to interweave with an old wall. To the left, high above the plantations enshrouding the clutch of reservoirs, is a big skyline of Twizle Head Moss and Herbage Edge beyond Holme Moss, with Black Hill ahead. **The path reaches an old gateway on a brow, with a plantation up to the left and the village of Holme just ahead.** Down the valley beyond Holmfirth rises the more solid Emley Moor TV mast.

The path curves round to the right, through reedy terrain in company with an old wall, then drops to a stile giving access to another colourful clough, that of Rake Dike. The path falls steeply to Gill Hey footbridge in lovely surrounds. An old made way slants back up the other side, quickly leaving the trees and continuing, reasonably clearly, through several fields to a small gate in front of a house at the far corner. Up the garden side is a kissing-gate onto a driveway, rising onto the A6024 in Holme, rather neatly opposite the *Fleece Inn*. For a note on Holme see page 57.

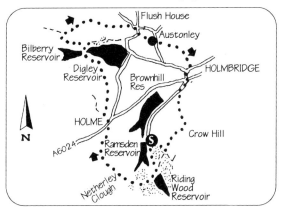

Turn right just as far as the cobbled square, and then up through it and along the no-through-road. Note a 1696 datestone on the arch at the small playground entrance. **As the road bends left to rise towards the school, turn right along an inviting, grassy walled way. On expiring cross the field to a stile at the foot of the opposite wall, then continue above a wall, with Digley Reservoir appearing in front. The path then crosses a string of pastures linked by a mix of traditional and modern stiles. The way remains reasonably clear, occasionally slanting right as Digley Reservoir becomes a major feature. Some maps incorrectly show the latter stage, as the path drops down onto a broad permissive path arriving from the reservoir's south car park.**

Turn left on the broad path, taking a stile on the right into a colourful heather and bilberry tract near the reservoir. The path drops to the very head of the reservoir, which is also the embankment of the freshly revealed Bilberry Reservoir. This is a charming spot, looking across the smaller reservoir to the steep-walled Marsden and Hey Cloughs. Bilberry Reservoir's engaging character belies its gruesome past, however, for this calm oasis was the scene of a major disaster in 1852. Following a torrential cloudburst on the moors, its dam burst and a swollen torrent raced down the valley, taking 81 lives with it.

Across the embankment a track slants away, doubling back right up to a junction of like tracks by a seat on some open ground. Take the branch doubling back left, soon turning to climb to a T-junction, where turn right. This broad track is Shay Lane, which leads out onto the surfaced Acres Lane. Its fine course looks down on Digley Reservoir and beyond to the Holme Valley's moorland skyline. At the road advance the few yards to a crossroads, and turn right a few more yards down to a stile on the left at a bend. In addition to the adjacent Digley Reservoir and its small neighbour, there are glimpses of both Brownhill and Ramsden Reservoirs to the south.

From the stile slant across the field to a stile opposite, then down the wallside to a stile below. Turn left to approach the large house at Austonley, where a stile sees the path outside its grounds, along to another stile to join its drive at a road, Roods Lane. Looking back, the house is a curious architectural hybrid, the central of three distinctly different aged sections being the oldest. Cross straight over Roods Lane and along behind another house, where a walled grassy way is enjoyed to its demise. Don't enter the field but take a stile on the left, and follow the right-hand wall declining gently away. Remain with this wall as good stiles lead through three fields to a path crossroads, where parallel walls run away to the left. Ignore these and the stile in front, and turn right down the facing wallside, bound for the modern housing of Holmbridge in the valley below.

After descending two fields the route transfers to the left side of a wall to reach the rear of some gardens. From a stile at the bottom, go right a couple of yards to a gate where the path squeezes between gardens onto a suburban street. Cross straight over and down in similar fashion to emerge via steps onto a road in Holmbridge. The pub is just to the left, while a final flight of steps leads down to the A6024 alongside the Post office and opposite the church.

Unassuming Holmbridge is based around the confluence of similar sized valleys in the upper Holme Valley, those of Marsden Clough and the river Holme itself. Centrepiece is the imposing church of St. David - or the *Bridge Tavern*, depending on your persuasion. **Turn right to cross the bridge and go left along a side road signed to Yate Holme. When it splits take the right branch, Bank Lane.** Set into the wall on the left is an old well, initialled and dated 1834. **The road becomes Brownhill Lane as it climbs past a restaurant to a junction.**

At once turn left up the side of some houses, on an access road rising to a short terrace. Take a kissing-gate to the right, across the garden to another gate into the foot of a narrow enclosure. Rise straight up this in company with a tiny stream, rapidly unfolding into a splendid wooded clough complete with a good path on the left, high above the stream. It ends abruptly at the top, where an old sunken way zigzags up to the right. Towards the field top, a fainter slant to the right leads up to a stile/gate onto a walled green way under Crow Hill. Look back over the dam of Brownhill Reservoir, with Digley Reservoir beyond it beneath Wessenden Head Moor.

Turn right along the path, and ignoring an immediate branch climbing left, remain with the right-hand wall. The main way slowly angles down along the base of these rough pastures, enjoying fine views to the valley head. It continues to slant down to the top corner of a wood. Entering at a stile, a broad path turns down the near side to drop back down to the car park.

Netherley Clough

15

HOLME VALLEY

START Holmfirth   Grid ref. SE 141081

DISTANCE 4½ miles

ORDNANCE SURVEY MAPS
1:50,000
Landranger 110 - Sheffield & Huddersfield
1:25,000
Outdoor Leisure 1 - Peak District, Dark Peak

ACCESS Start from the town centre. Central car parks. Served by bus from Huddersfield and also from Marsden, Meltham, Wakefield, Penistone and Barnsley; seasonal services from Glossop and Buxton.

Simple and delightful: hamlets and cloughs, old fieldpaths and lanes.

S Holmfirth is the principal town of the Holme Valley in its journey from Holme Moss to Huddersfield. It is a characterful place whose nooks and crannies well merit a leisurely potter. The unusual parish church of the Holy Trinity replaced one damaged in the flood of 1777. For decades Holmfirth was best known for the saucy seaside postcards produced by Bamforths: the town boasts a Postcard Museum and even a *Postcard* pub. Less well known is that Bamforths were pioneers of silent films long before Hollywood became the place to be! For the last quarter-century, it has been the antics of a trio of juvenile pensioners in TV's *Last of the Summer Wine* that have put Holmfirth on the map.

From the junction of Victoria Street with the main road in the town centre, go left a short way to the Tourist Information Centre. Just past it, before the Library, turn up a pathway which climbs into the sloping Victoria Park. Stay on the main setted path which curves up to the right, and from the top corner a snicket runs out onto a road, Cooper Lane. Turn up this to the T-junction just ahead.

Go right a few yards and turn up a path squeezing between gardens. It winds very steeply up through trees to run out between drives onto an access road at Hill. Go left, leaving the houses behind to effect a rapid move into the countryside. The rough road of Hill Lane continues as a walled track between the fields. Over to the right are first views down the valley to the prominent tower on Castle Hill above Huddersfield. **The track runs unfailingly on to enter Upperthong at a sharp bend in the road.** Standing at around 920ft/280m, this hilltop village has been much enlarged by modern housing. It was an old weaving settlement, and a prominent reminder is the three-storeyed Weavers House on the main street. **Head straight along this main street, Towngate, passing the *Royal Oak* pub to arrive at a junction with Wickens Lane at the far end.**

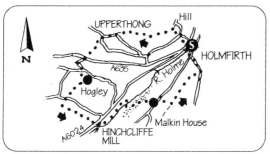

Bear left, down through another sharp bend out of the village. This heralds a spacious view as the whole of the upper Holme Valley opens out, dominated by the mass of Black Hill with the Holme Moss TV mast prominent. **Within yards take a stile on the right, and cross the field centre to the next one. From this turn down the wallside to a stile onto a rough lane. Go right on this, dropping down past the house at Newlands, with a 1746 datestone and mullioned windows, to emerge onto the A635 Greenfield road.**

Cross with care and go straight down Black Sike Lane opposite, into wooded Hart Holes Clough and steeply up the other side to a junction, where turn right. Note at once the old stone hut bearing an Austonley Local Board Waterworks 1889 tablet. **Just beyond, as the road opens out at Hogley Green, turn left along a driveway, and keep left at a fork to pass between houses and along to the old hamlet of Hogley. Swing right between the buildings to a gate/stile out into a field. Head away with the wall, crossing to the left side at the corner**

stile and resuming. From the next stile drop across the field centre to one opposite, then advance with a wall down to a stile onto **Cold Well Lane**, at a nice corner where a stone slab bridges a tiny stream.

Go right just as far as the lone house. The key to its origin is etched above the door: *This school built by subscription 1816.* **A grassy pathway turns down its far side, swinging pleasantly down to a gate/ kissing-gate before a sharp bend at a path junction. Ignore the stile in the corner and turn left down this broad enclosed way, dropping gently to reach a gate/stile at the head of a wooded clough. The path resumes as a splendid grassy way above the edge of the clough, running down to join a drive. Down to the left is a large millpond. Don't follow the drive down through the houses, but cross straight over, quickly turning left through a stile between houses at Upper Stubbin. Entering a field, a largely stone surfaced path descends to a stile at the bottom, from where a driveway, Stubbin Lane, runs straight down to Woodhead Road (A6024) at Hinchcliffe Mill.**

Cross straight over and bear left along Old Road to an angled crossroads. A fine assortment of old houses are passed, including three-storeyed weavers' dwellings and a contrastingly squat single-storey terrace. **At the end go straight ahead on Water Street.** Strung along this mill road are old millworkers' cottages still sharing the millowners' choice of paintwork. **Into the yard keep straight on past the end of the mill itself, to a footbridge on the river Holme. Don't cross, but head downstream on a path between the mill-race and the river.** This runs on through wooded surrounds as the watercourse opens out into a sizeable millpond backed by a large mill at Burnlee.

Before the end of the pond, drop down to a bridge on the adjacent river. Ignoring a direct path up into the woods, double back a few yards upstream. When the path forks bear left up the pasture to a path crossroads before the trees, then turn left up the path to an old stile into the wood. Turning left the path immediately forks. Bear right up through the trees, slanting through a cutting immediately beneath an old quarry site. Crossing a level path, the slanting path continues up to a stile at the woodtop just above, this upper section being dense with hollies.

The path continues slanting across two fields to the prominent Malkin House ahead. This proves to be a splendid three-storeyed weaver's house in a lovely setting. **Pass straight up the drive, through**

this old hamlet and onto a back road, Brow Lane, where turn left.
This affords the most direct return to Holmfirth, with glorious views
over the valley. En route, barns on the left include a 1752 initialled
datestone, with a fine series of stone troughs at the foot of grassy Ward
Place Lane up to the abandoned settlement on the right.

**Better, however, to leave the road within yards by a stile (right), and
turn up the wallside. The faint path slants left from the corner above,
up to another corner stile, then more clearly to a stile above a stone
hut. This accesses an old walled way.** Along here, *Summer Wine*
devotees will be fully expecting to see Compo-like characters ambling
along. **Turn left down this rough track, passing above an old weaving
settlement of some pedigree, sadly derelict. The track, Ward Bank
Road, runs on past several seats to linger over this final section's
views before curving round to drop down onto Cartworth Road.**

**Turn left to re-enter Holmfirth. As it becomes Rotcher Road there is
an option to drop left down steps onto the
back lane of Goose Green, which can
also be left lower down by a snicket
on the left to reach the bridge on
Hollowgate, crossing it to join
the main road.** Note the old
milestone set into the bridge,
and the old tollbooth, now
a bookshop on the left.
**The start is just
along to the
right.**

Weavers House,
Upperthong

16

MELTHAM MOOR

START Meltham   Grid ref. SE 099106

DISTANCE 6¾ miles

ORDNANCE SURVEY MAPS
1:50,000
Landranger 110 - Sheffield & Huddersfield
1:25,000
Outdoor Leisure 1 - Peak District, Dark Peak
Outdoor Leisure 21 - South Pennines (tiny section only)

ACCESS Start from the central junction near the church. There is a car park up Clarke Lane behind the centrally placed Rose & Crown pub. Buses from Huddersfield. • ACCESS NOTE: the walk includes two sections of concessionary path linking West Nab with Wessenden Head Road. Negotiated with Meltham Shooting Club, the paths can be closed at times of shooting and high fire risk, when it would then be necessary to omit West Nab and remain on the road.

A bracing tramp in the northern extremities of Peakland, interspersed with colourful side valleys.

❺ Meltham is an unassuming West Riding settlement, a cross between a large village and a small town. Though in many ways independent it is served by Huddersfield for all major purposes. St. Bartholomew's church with its tall spire dominates the centre. Note also the Carlile Institute. There is a large Odd Fellows Hall of 1851. **Take the road round the back of the church and turn off up Colders Lane between some housing. This rises away, and at the top becomes a narrow lane past older houses. This then quickly transforms into a narrow footpath to escape from suburbia. Rising between walls it emerges onto a road, Leygards Lane.** Straight ahead is the edge of Meltham Moor.

Go left to a crossroads with the Greenfield road, and straight over onto a broad farm drive. Now we have fine views back over the town, featuring Meltham Cop, Castle Hill and the Emley Moor TV mast. **The track passes over a drain to suddenly emerge on the edge of Royd Edge Clough.** This is a splendid moment: at our feet is the sweeping, colourful clough, its heather-clad flanks rising to a broad skyline of Meltham Moor.

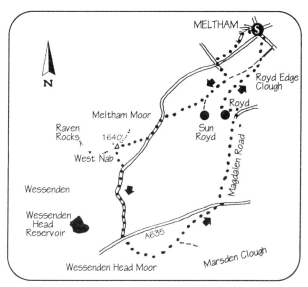

Turn right on the clough-side track, and at a gate at the top leave the track going left down to Sun Royd Farm, and continue straight up with the wall. A brief spell in the fields follows until moorland returns, remaining up the wallside to emerge onto Wessenden Head Road on the open moor. With the rocks of West Nab just above, head up the road for five minutes to a path branching right. A notice advises that this is a negotiated concessionary path off which there is no access. **The path crosses a fence-stile to rise pleasantly across the moor, slanting up to gain the edge just short of West Nab.** At 1640ft/500m this high point of the moor is also the highest point reached in these walks. It is crowned by an Ordnance Survey column amongst a scattering of large gritstone boulders. Arrival here is truly a superb moment, with an outstanding panorama in all directions.

From this position on the edge of one National Park we can see into the next one up the Pennines, with Penyghent and Great Whernside notable landmarks in the Yorkshire Dales. Rolling moorlands include Black Hill to the south and a long sweep of the Saddleworth, Marsden and Calderdale moors to north and west. Man's efforts at piercing the skyline cannot be ignored either: diverse features include transmitter masts on Emley Moor and Holme Moss and windfarms at Coal Clough (above Todmorden) and Ovenden Moor (above Halifax), while the monument on Stoodley Pike adds a more endearing element to man's efforts. Buckstones, Blackstone Edge and Pendle Hill restore sanity.

From West Nab the route was planned to follow a thin path westwards atop a minor edge to the characterful grouping of Raven Rocks, where at a stile to their south-east the end of the concession path meets the boundary of National Trust access land: Leyzing Clough would have led to the Pennine Way in Wessenden. However, adhering to the Trust's policy not to encourage increased use of the moor, the route is amended as follows, taking advantage of another concession path.

From the trig. point head south, leaving the boulders for a steep drop towards Wessenden Head Road. In clear weather the Holme Moss mast is a perfect directional guide, while part way down the slope a faint path materialises with the aid of occasional marker posts. At the bottom a fence-stile sees the path across moister ground onto the road. Turn right, passing a boundary stone and tracing a quiet course across the moors with Wessenden down to the right. Seen below is Wessenden Head Reservoir, completed in 1881 and the highest of four in the valley. Beyond it is Wessenden Head Moor and ahead is Black Hill, while looking back, West Nab casts a shapely profile.

Absorbing the reservoir's access road, the Pennine Way is also briefly joined. This section of the Way was originally merely the 'Wessenden alternative', but is now put forward as the definitive route to avoid and protect the excesses of juicy moorland on the watershed. **A couple of minutes further, the A635 is reached at Wessenden Head.** At one time the celebrated *Isle of Skye* pub welcomed travellers to this isolated spot, but was demolished in the 1950s on the pretext that water gathering grounds might become polluted.

Almost on the junction, just to the left, a ladder-stile takes a path onto Wessenden Head Moor. Slanting faintly left it quickly becomes clearer and runs down the moor as a fine grassy path. Straight ahead, the PW can be seen coming down off Black Hill. **At a wall corner the path turns left and remains a grand route, becoming partly enclosed and running above a scattered wood. After crossing a colourful clough it runs on to a hairpin bend on a broad track, Springs Road: turn left up this.** While admiring the view over Marsden Clough, Digley Reservoir and the upper Holme Valley, also note the two laned causeyed way beneath our feet. The well defined grooves in the stones were formed by the wheels of horse-drawn carts heavily laden with stone from the quarries, some of which are right by the path.

At the end the old way rises back onto the main road. Go right a few yards to a gate opposite, and another bridleway (Magdalen Road) heads off up the wall-side. Back onto moorland, it soon attains the brow. Here we earn a splendid picture of the first stage of the walk, over Royd Edge Clough. **The way then descends the moor-side as a grand path, becoming enclosed as a broad green way at the bottom corner. Quickly absorbing a farm drive (Ash Royd), continue down to a bend before the next farm, then take a gate on the left. A grassy, partly marshy old drive runs down to the forlorn ruin of Royd.**

Turn through an old gateway on the right after a barn before the main building, and head down with a wall on the right. Through another old wall our thin trod enters colourful terrain almost at the bottom of the clough. Birch trees enshroud the stream, while our way contours around just above. There is a popular local footpath shadowing the stream to which one might descend directly. The public footpath meanwhile continues on above, through another old wall and then slants down to a hurdle-stile in the corner. All of this neighbourhood is very attractive indeed.

Here the stream is crossed to gain that parallel path. Turn downstream, and at a near immediate fork either remain on the bottom path till deflected up above a millpond, or at the first chance fork up to the left. At a crossroads with a contouring path turn right to run along to the edge of the clough. The broader path merges from down to the right, and a cobbled road is met in front of a cottage. Go left up the cobbles, quickly out along a road, Hebble Lane. Meeting another lane at Laithe Farm, descend a few feet then take a kissing-gate on the left. Along a field bottom the path negotiates between modern housing, crossing straight over a suburban road and on to the next street, Tinker Lane, where it ends. Turn down to the right to finish, emerging onto the main road just short of the centre.

17

WESSENDEN

START *Marsden*   *Grid ref. SE 047116*

DISTANCE *7 miles*

ORDNANCE SURVEY MAPS
1:50,000
Landranger 110 - Sheffield & Huddersfield
1:25,000
Outdoor Leisure 1 - Peak District, Dark Peak
Outdoor Leisure 21 - South Pennines

ACCESS *Start from Towngate, outside the parish church. Reasonable parking in the vicinity. Served by bus from Huddersfield, Holmfirth and Oldham and by train from Huddersfield and Manchester.*

An exploration of the northernmost valley in the Peak District, where the South Pennines indefinably merge, and a breezy moorland return.

S   For a note on Marsden see page 78. **From the church cross Towngate to a little green with stocks, then along a path over the stream and into the Market Place. Advance to the front of the Mechanics Hall, then turn right past the shops up Peel Street. Cross the main road (A62) at the top and continue up the next road. Go left a few yards then take a drive doubling back uphill. At the top, ending at two houses, stay on the right, through a private-looking gate to the farm. Go left into the yard to find a stile on the right at the end. This admit to contrastingly open country as a sunken way rises up to moorland slopes.** There are now grand views back over the town, with Pule Hill and Buckstones high above.

The old way slants up to the right then along to a fork: the level path goes straight on over a stile, while our branch slants up left with an old wall, again in very pronounced sunken fashion. It continues up

to meet a stile above a stone hut. Super views now reach over the Wessenden Valley to the moors. Below us is Butterley Reservoir, completed in 1906 as the last of the valley's four reservoirs, and by far the largest. **The path continues rising across a slimmer enclosure to the next stile, through which it meets a firm drive on the edge of the National Trust's Binn Moor. Go right on this, slanting down before running on to a junction with a narrow road. Go left on here for a short half-mile, serving several houses before suddenly losing its surface at the last one.**

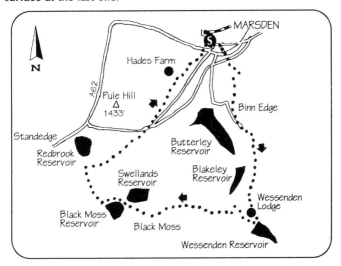

Just a few yards further the track also ends, leaving a path to take over. Further grand views see Wessenden's two lower reservoirs below. **The path immediately forks: take the right one, slanting down through open country to a stone bridge in Rams Clough. Rising up the other side take a stile on the right to enter green pastures. Indicated by stiles throughout, advance to the next one then on the field top to a dip before a prominent green path slants down to the far corner gateway. The way then runs on by a wallside and past a low ruin to cross a tiny clough, ambitiously named Great Clough. Press on by another ruin and with another old wall. Slant down to a fence-stile and on again to a second one, by which time the trees enshrouding Wessenden Lodge are in view ahead.** Over to the right our route out of the valley can be seen climbing by Blakely Clough.

Advance on through a further stile to the left of a gate (not quite as per map), crossing the mini-clough of Hey Dike and across a lush pasture to the wall along the back of the farm. Keep straight on through a further stile to meet a broad path by the dam of Wessenden Reservoir. The valley's oldest reservoir was built as long ago as 1790 to operate waterwheels in the Colne Valley, and enlarged 50 years later. Here we join the Pennine Way: for many years merely the 'Wessenden alternative', this is now put forward as the definitive route to avoid and protect the excesses of juicy moorland on the watershed.

Turn down a few yards to a bridge over the outflow. Currently there is no right of way over the embankment, even though regularly used by PW walkers, continuing away on a path into Small Clough. A stone hut, weirs and a waterfall are found within its confines: the path negotiates the stream beneath the fall, and contours out to another water installation. The right of way continues down the rough road, which is soon left by a steep path doubling back down to a footbridge on Wessenden Brook. It climbs back up the other side to meet the contouring path. This offers a view down over Blakeley Reservoir, smallest of Wessenden's four. The level path swings in to cross Blakely Clough then climbs onto the moor, rising pleasantly with the diminishing clough onto the peaty heights. Looking back, Raven Rocks on Meltham Moor top the skyline above Wessenden Lodge.

On levelling out, Pennine Way paving takes over for an easy march all the way to Black Moss Reservoir. Just beneath it is neighbouring Swellands Reservoir, with Pule Hill and Buckstones beyond. Both the reservoirs, along with the soon to be seen Redbrook Reservoir, were built to supply water for the Huddersfield Narrow Canal. A grassy path crosses the low embankment to a seat and tiny beach at the other corner. It then runs on a little further to swing left to a junction with the PW's original route above the main embankment.

Turning right the flags immediately return to rise to a modest brow on Rocher Moss. Here the view westwards over steep flanks into the Saddleworth area is replaced by Redbrook Reservoir appearing below. The path remains flagged as it descends the moorland of Bobus to meet a broad, contouring path at a breached embankment. This was the second turnpike road over Standedge, completed in 1815, and its firmer course is now taken advantage of by yet another re-aligned section of the PW. While the PW goes left, take the pitched path on the other side of the gap and head along to the right. Prime feature of the view now is Pule Hill just to our left. **Our track soon begins a steady descent of the moor to join Mount Road.** By-passing Marsden to the south, Mount Road was the main turnpike route across Standedge prior to the building of the present A62 to the north of Pule Hill in 1839.

Descend a little further on the road to a junction with Old Mount Road. As its name suggests, this was the first turnpike route created by the celebrated Blind Jack of Knaresborough around 1759, on the line of a packhorse trail. **Go left here, and almost at once bear left along the Hades farm drive. This runs on for some time along the moor edge.** Down below is the golf course backed by the entrance to Wessenden, and on the skyline the Raven Rocks on Meltham Moor. Hades Farm had a brief spell as a youth hostel in the early 1970s.

Ignoring paths branching down to the right, keep on until the drive swings around to the left. Here advance the short way down to a gate in a corner of the moor. Through it, an old sunken way winds down between crumbling walls. It affords fine views over Marsden and its environs, centred very much on the church. **The way descends pleasantly to a fine old house featuring mullioned windows. Enter the yard and go left of the buildings to a gate at the bottom. Descend the field on a hugely deep-set hollow way, winding down to a stile in the corner. Just below, a house drive leads down to the right to Old Mount Road. Go left to the Towngate junction with the main road.**

For a nice finish go left on the main road to the end of the church-yard, then descend a path onto the road at Clough Lea. Noting the arched Mellor Bridge (dating from 1772 with origins in packhorse days) go right on the streamside lane past attractive cottages to return to Towngate.

Small Clough,
Wessenden

⟨ 18 ⟩

STANDEDGE CLASSIC

START *Standedge*   *Grid ref. SE 018094*

DISTANCE *6¾ miles*

ORDNANCE SURVEY MAPS
1:50,000
Landranger 110 - Sheffield & Huddersfield
1:25,000
Outdoor Leisure 1 - Peak District, Dark Peak
Outdoor Leisure 21 - South Pennines

ACCESS *Start from Brun Clough Reservoir car park on the top of the A62 at Standedge, just east of the Floating Light pub. Served by Oldham-Huddersfield buses.*

A memorable combination of moorland ways, from packhorse trails and old turnpikes to a celebrated walkers' highway.

❺ The small dam of Brun Clough Reservoir was one of many built to supply the Huddersfield Narrow Canal (see WALK 19). **From the car park cross the road and follow the Pennine Way northwards along a rising path.** At once there are fine views left down into Saddleworth. **The way quickly swings left as a broad firm track, and in a minor cutting the PW is signed off to the right over a stile. An inviting path rises across moor grass slopes.** Over to the right rises Pule Hill, with Shooters Nab and West Nab on the more distant skyline to its right.

Just before a first stile in a crumbling wall, leave the PW on a path curving away to the right, crossing various tracks on its short course to a fence-stile into National Trust land on Close Moss. We are on the route of the area's first turnpike road, built in 1759 by the celebrated John Metcalfe (Blind Jack of Knaresborough), and shall very shortly encounter a remarkable survivor from that time. **Advance straight**

along an improving grassy path, on a gentle decline to Thieves
Clough Bridge. This stone arched structure makes a splendid sight in
the midst of sombre moorland, almost a bizarre apparition reached as
it is by no more than a grassy track. As we descend from the moor here,
our route is also on the line of a Roman road.

Just a little further down another National Trust sign is reached in
front of spoil heaps which surround a tall, imposing stone building.
Happily preserved, this is an engine winding house which helped
extract spoil during construction of Standedge Tunnel. Behind it is the
now dominant crest of Pule Hill above the *Carriage House* pub on the
A62: we are looking straight up to the heart of Pule Hill's quarry.

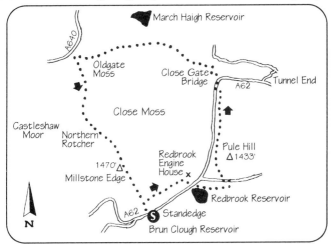

Go right over a tiny stream and a path shadows an old catchwater
round to the A62 at the *Great Northern* pub. Cross over and along
Redbrook Reservoir's grassy dam. Over the outflow keep straight on
a thin trod, soon meeting a catchwater near a tiny arched bridge. The
path traces a low embankment alongside it until it turns sharp right,
then the path angles down to the left towards the adjacent Mount
Road. At a cross-path turn left to conveniently gain the road summit.
Double back left for 150 yards and turn right along an inviting grassy
path along the base of Pule Hill. This is Boat Lane, the route by which
canal ponies were led over Standedge to Diggle while their boats
were 'legged' through the three-mile tunnel far below.

The steep slopes above lead to Pule Hill's 1433ft/437m top. Features of its extensive view include West Nab on Meltham Moor, and Holme Moss TV mast and Black Hill beyond Wessenden's reservoirs; Black Moss and Swellands reservoirs by the Pennine Way to the south; Redbrook Reservoir under Standedge Cutting with greater Manchester beyond; a big moorland sweep to the north, over Buckstones to Windy Hill mast overlooking the unseen M62; north-east then east over the Colne Valley, including part of Marsden, Slaithwaite and beyond towards Huddersfield, Castle Hill with its tower and Emley Moor with its taller if less inspiring TV mast. Those tempted by a clear day's prospects could rejoin the route by going north along the edge, then doubling back down a grassy track when the rocks abate.

The main path runs a fine course beneath Pule Hill's craggy edge on the line of the 'Standedge Trail' highlighted on the map, which runs in and out of National Trust land on agreed paths. The path runs on to adjacent rising grassy ways. Both served the old quarries up above, the first being an incline down which stone was carried, and the second an access track. **Advance straight on, now faintly, passing round the base of a big spoil heap, a few yards down a descending track, then on again to a wall-gap ahead.** Very close below is the A62, where motorists are regularly alarmed by bold (or foolish) sheep opting to sit in the middle of the road. **Now pathless, keep straight on to slant a little down to a stile back into NT land. With the *Coach & Horses* pub just below, head on again to a white house at Owlers. Just past a second house, take a ladder-stile on the left and down a tiny fieldside to a stile onto the road. Cross and follow the footway right.**

At the bend turn down a walled grassy footway on the left, soon dropping steeply to Redbrook Clough. Cross and turn right a few yards along the foot of the moor to Close Gate Bridge, a beautiful structure overlooking a confluence in a delightful setting. This outstanding packhorse bridge is better known as Eastergate Bridge, a corruption of Esther's Gate, named after the landlady of the *Packhorse Inn* that stood nearby.

Without crossing, head away on the main path by Haigh Clough. We are now on the Rapes Highway, a splendid packhorse route. Trains of pack-ponies would have regularly toiled along here during the 17th and 18th centuries carrying goods, principally wool, between Marsden and Milnrow. The route is lined by marker posts inscribed *PH Road*, erected in 1908 by Marsden Town Council. **Within yards the path**

turns to climb steeply out of the foot of Stonepit Lee Clough. The stream in Willykay Clough is soon crossed above a small waterfall before a gentler climb across Close Moss. The Buckstones skyline features to the north. This infallible course leads steadily up onto Oldgate Moss, across which the A640 Rochdale-Huddersfield road is joined on its bleak moorland crest. Virtually at once the Pennine Way comes in from the left, so it's straight back onto the moor, across Haigh Gutter to follow this famous route southwards. Before long the path curves right to gain the start of the gritstone edge of Northern Rotcher: a stone marker post signals our merging with the more recently devised Oldham Way. Below is the Castleshaw Valley with its twin reservoirs, backed by the Saddleworth scene. A splendid stride now heads along the crest of the scarp.

When the rocks abate the path runs on to approach the shorter-lived grouping at Millstone Edge. The route passes the flat-topped Dinner Stone to arrive at the concrete Ordnance Survey column, at 1470ft/ 448m the summit of the walk. Almost at the walk's end this is very much a stage to savour as the weathered rock formations look down on Diggle and southwards to the hills above Saddleworth. Just before it, identified by a cairn above is a memorial stone recalling Ammon Wrigley, local poet and Saddleworth expert. Resuming, the path drops gently to a wall-stile off the moor proper, and down through stiles in old walls amid rough pastures. The last one returns us to the moorland where the walk began, with Brun Clough Reservoir and its car park just below. Retrace the outward steps to finish.

*Redbrook
Engine House
and Pule Hill*

(19)

BUCKSTONES

START Marsden　　　　Grid ref. SE 046118

DISTANCE 7 miles

ORDNANCE SURVEY MAPS
1:50,000
Landranger 110 - Sheffield & Huddersfield
1:25,000
Outdoor Leisure 21 - South Pennines

ACCESS Start from outside the railway station. Served by train from Huddersfield and Manchester, and bus from Huddersfield, Holmfirth, Oldham. Parking outside the station and at various places in the town.

A magnificent walk through the heart of the National Trust's Marsden Moor estate. While these sweeping moorlands are designated open access, this route remains on public rights of way in order to lessen disturbance to ground nesting birds.

S Marsden is the first settlement in the Colne Valley, which runs an increasingly populated course down into Huddersfield. Large textile mills and terraced rows typify this once manufacturing dominated town, and the Colne Valley was a hotbed of unrest when the Luddite movement was in full ferment. Near the old stocks on the green outside the church is the tomb of Enoch Taylor, a machine-maker at the heart of the troubles: those who feared the machines would take their jobs famously gave his name to the tools they used to smash them, and just four miles away, award-winning Linfit Brewery brews the strong 'Enoch's Hammer'. Indeed, Marsden has its own tiny, centrally sited brewery.

Sheltering in a great bowl of the Pennines beneath Pule Hill, Marsden has much of interest. St. Bartholomew's church dominates the centre, set at a respectable distance from the modest little shopping streets. Alongside is shapely Mellor Bridge, dating from 1772 but with its origins in packhorse times.

At the station entrance take a gate giving access to the Huddersfield Narrow Canal at a lock. Go left/west on the towpath, a pleasant amble opposite heathery banks before passing under low-slung railway bridges to arrive at the old basin. Opposite stands a former warehouse, now unused. **The towpath rises to a bridge at Tunnel End, a focal point of the canal featuring a Canal and Countryside Centre at Tunnel End Cottages.**

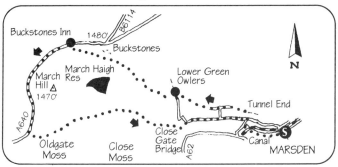

The Huddersfield Narrow Canal was built to convey goods such as coal, lime, stone and textiles between towns on either side of the Pennines. It links with the Huddersfield Broad Canal at Apsley Basin near Huddersfield, and the Ashton Canal at Dukinfield near Ashton-under-Lyne, a total length of 19½ miles. Work began in 1794, and within five years 42 locks helped it ascend 436ft to Marsden on the east, and (ultimately) 32 locks the 334ft on the west to Diggle. Then came the impasse of Standedge, fraught with engineering and financial difficulties: the construction of the highest, deepest and (at more than three miles) the longest canal tunnel in the land was, ultimately, a magnificent achievement for the age.

Until establishing this connection in 1811, goods had to be unloaded at either end and carried over Standedge. On completion the canal horses would still have to be led over the top while the boatmen 'legged' their way through the tunnel. This crude method of progress required the men to sit and work their feet along the wall of the 8ft wide canal. Sadly the waterway's death knell sounded early, when in the 1840s the canal company was bought out by a railway company. While work on the rail tunnels started in 1846, the canal survived well into the 20th century. When the tunnel finally closed in 1944, it had been unnavigable for some years, and by that time no-one could have foreseen any future for the Huddersfield Narrow Canal.

In 1974, with just six locks remaining open, enthusiasts of the newly formed Huddersfield Canal Society could only dream of what might be achieved. Hard graft and dedication saw steady progress on tasks such as restoring locks, dredging and general repair work. However, several major obstacles were always going to appear insurmountable, from creating brand new sections of canal, to the inevitable problem of Standedge Tunnel. Enlisting the co-operation of local authorities and British Waterways was a major step in the 1980s, and ultimately a massive grant ensured that achievement of the 'impossible dream' was just a matter of time. The year 2001 sees the restored Standedge Tunnel herald the culmination of a remarkable restoration programme.

The railway, meanwhile, runs a parallel course under Standedge, and the railway company decided on two tunnels. The first was completed in 1848, and at just over three miles it became the world's longest rail tunnel. Advantage of the canal tunnel was taken in order to remove the spoil by boat, thus saving a fortune. The companion tunnel was not completed until 1871, having been abandoned for 20 years in between. By the late 19th century increasing demands on the railways brought about the construction of a third tunnel. Completed in 1894 and this time double track, this is now the only one in use.

Cross the bridge and head away up the road to a junction in front of the *Tunnel End Inn*. Climb straight past it on a path alongside a driveway, the path continuing up past a house to meet an access road. Turn left on this rough road past several dwellings. It offers grand views ahead over the uppermost Colne Valley backed by the big sweep of the moorland estate. **The road becomes surfaced: on reaching a fork don't drop left but take that maintaining a higher course to two more houses. It ends abruptly just before the last one where an enclosed footway takes over. A little beyond the house it emerges into open pastures to advance invitingly away. Part-way on it turns up an obvious slant before running to a bridle-gate in a fence.** This affords a first view ahead to the Buckstones' moorland skyline, with the eponymous pub prominent. The drone of traffic is not the A640 at Buckstones, but the M62 motorway a good two miles distant.

From here the faint path drops a little, winding round to the right and on past a ruinous farm. Its old track drops to a stream crossing, where double briefly back, then climb the tree-lined wallside to a gate at the top. Joining a narrow road turn right, past a white house and down to a fork at Green Owlers Clough. Looking back over it, shapely Pule Hill fronts a different moorland skyline. Here turn left on the rough road running above the clough and on the moor edge to Hatter Lee. Continue past the house on a grassy track heading off through reeds in the direction of our objective, the skyline *Buckstones Inn*.

Striking away from the wall Haigh Clough appears ahead, with the grassy embankment of March Haigh Reservoir ahead beneath the knoll of March Hill. Approaching a sidestream, leave this path and bear right towards a crumbling wall corner. Now start to bear left up the pathless slope of March Haigh Flat, with steeper slopes above. With no visible path it is a matter of faith whether a hidden ruinous sheepfold is located on a shelf beneath steeper slopes. From here a path slants up the bank to the left, runs on past a spring and then fades a little: remember the target of the *Buckstones Inn*. Little more than a vague sheeptrod, it runs a largely level course, through a few rocks and some bracken.

Directly below is March Haigh Reservoir, and beyond Close Moss is Redbrook Reservoir to the right of Pule Hill, with both Holme Moss and Emley Moor TV masts in evidence. Both of the reservoirs were built by the Huddersfield Canal Company in the mid 1800s.

Buckstones

Increasingly prominent up above are the Buckstones, a typically inviting gritstone edge (though not seen to best advantage from below). Just above them is a parking area where the B6114 branches off the A640 Rochdale road. Here a National Trust board introduces Buckstones Edge to motorists, who from 1480ft/451m can effortlessly survey the greater part of the 5685 acre Marsden Moor estate. **Though still faint the grassy path picks up amid denser bracken , and a gentle rise across the slopes leads it to emerge onto the A640 in front of the isolated *Buckstones Inn*. Turn left for a mile of road walking, though with reasonable verges, excellent views and only limited traffic. An old milestone is passed at the head of Tom Clough, and the road continues round to meet a clear path coming in on the left.**

Double back on the path, which runs a gentle course onto the crest of Oldgate Moss. This old track is the Rapes Highway, a classic example of an old packhorse route. Trains of pack-ponies would have regularly toiled along this route over the Pennine watershed during the 17th and 18th centuries carrying goods, principally wool, between Marsden and Milnrow. The route is lined by marker posts inscribed *PH Road*, erected in 1908 by Marsden Town Council to confirm the status of this fine way after a dispute with the moor's then owner, the Lord of the Manor of Marsden.

The path is infallible as it descends Broad Wham and runs gently down across the moor, quickly crossing Willmer Green Clough. Now difficult to visualise is the scene of devastation here after a major moorland fire in the mid 1990s, for the extensive damage has been eradicated by the efforts of the National Trust and a hard-working band of volunteers who restored much of the vegetation. **The path declines only gently with a good prospect of our outward route to the left. The stream in Willykay Clough is crossed above a little waterfall, then the way quickly drops more steeply to the base of the moor. The main Haigh Clough is joined for the final yards to arrive at Close Gate Bridge by a lovely watersmeet.** This outstanding old packhorse bridge is better known as Eastergate Bridge, a corruption of Esther's Gate, named after the landlady of an inn that stood nearby.

Leave the moor by crossing the bridge, and a path runs downstream to quickly rise onto Waters Road. Turn right to finish, a pleasant amble, especially the first half through a nice dean. This leads back to the *Tunnel End Inn*, so descend to Tunnel End to embrace the towpath again for the final ten minutes of the walk.

20

SLAITHWAITE MOOR

START Marsden   Grid ref. SE 046118

DISTANCE 4½ miles

ORDNANCE SURVEY MAPS
1:50,000
Landranger 110 - Sheffield & Huddersfield
1:25,000
Outdoor Leisure 21 - South Pennines

ACCESS Start from outside the railway station. Served by train from Huddersfield and Manchester, and bus from Huddersfield, Holmfirth, Oldham. Parking outside the station and at various places in the town.

A super mixture of moorland and canalside on some fine old trackways.

S For a note on Marsden see page 78. **From the station entrance by the *Railway* pub, turn right up to the road bridge over rail and canal. Across, turn right on Reddisher Road, briefly, then strike left up the steep and grassy Spring Head Lane. On easing out at a large house, bear right along a level, grassy cart track.** By this stage there are big views back over the town, with the Wessenden Valley striking away south into the moors. **The track runs on to the rear of several houses at Dirker, but before it becomes a rough lane, turn left up a more inviting sunken green way. This slants steeply up between walls, absorbing another such way to rise onto a rough drive at a farm.**

Cross to a stile above and continue up with the reedy sunken way. The going quickly levels out and the grassy track (Huck Hill Lane) runs on between old walls, a good stride as it leads unfailingly and now very gently up across increasingly rough pastures. With moorland slopes all around the transformation is complete, and as the right-hand wall disappears a moister section utilises much of the adjacent old wall to rise across **Netherwood Heys to a stile/gate in a fence at the wall corner. Continuing straight up, the improved path runs on through the rough heather and grass of Shaw Heys, part of the National Trust's Marsden Moor estate. It leaves their land to cross the tiny Old Clough by way of a similarly small bridge.**

Across a small marsh behind it the path rises gently across Slaithwaite Moor. In superb grassy condition the path quickly arrives at a junction by a memorial seat. At 1246ft/380m this marks the summit of the walk, and on a clear day it offers the ideal backrest to survey a fine view south over Shooters Nab, Black Hill, Wessenden, Pule Hill, Standedge and Marsden Moor. This also marks a junction of the Kirklees Way and the Colne Valley Circular Walk. By advancing a few yards further to the brow, Cupwith Reservoir appears just in front.

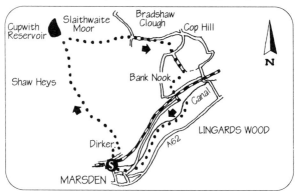

Our route now turns right on a similarly good path running east with a dike. Ahead, the tower on Castle Hill above Huddersfield is seen in front of the Emley Moor TV mast. **Passing shooting butts and a ruined stone hut the path leads to a stile off the moor. It continues along a fieldside to the head of a walled green way and out onto a cross-roads. Go straight ahead on Old Ground, as far as a patch of open ground on the right, with Wham Farm down to the left. Turn right on the wallside track at the end of the open patch, quickly bearing left with it to remain with the wall on the left. This rapidly transforms into a splendid grassy byway, Cop Hill Lane, as it runs between walls. When a lesser grassy way turns off left, advance just a few yards further to take a stile on the right. Cross the narrow field to a stile opposite, then descend a wallside onto a T-junction of back roads.**

Go straight down Green Lane opposite, and when it narrows and steepens to descend to the hamlet of Bank Nook, bear right along a cart track. This runs to an isolated house: pass along the front to a stile, and a part-walled grassy path heads away. From a stile at the end it slants down a little more to become a narrower path down through a sharp bend, then crossing a trickle to a moist area with another stream in front. A local quagmire in winter, plans are in hand for improvement work. Turn down, evading marshy patches and becoming fully enclosed to debouch onto Crow Trees Road.

Go straight ahead under the railway bridge and straight down the no-through-road of Kettle Lane in front. The continuing cart track passes between the houses at Booth to wind down to a bridge on the Huddersfield Narrow Canal. The towpath is joined at a lovely corner, with a holding basin where boats would queue for the lock, the scene completed by ducks and a cottage. One glance into the lock is sufficient to appreciate how the waterway got its name. For more on the canal see page 78.

Turn right for an uncomplicated return of just over a mile to the station at Marsden. En route a number of locks are passed as the canal makes its final ascent to its summit at Standedge Tunnel. Just beyond an old mill with a big circular stone chimney, water dominates the landscape as a big millpond on the left is joined by Sparth Reservoir on the right. Further, the river Colne appears below, with a mill-cut alongside as two stone arches send it off from the weir side. Passing under Marsden Lane the canal enters town and the church tower is seen just ahead, though Marsden proper is screened by a bank to arrive at the station after passing under two final bridges.

Huddersfield Narrow Canal, Booth

MERRY DALE

START *Slaithwaite*   *Grid ref. SE 079139*

DISTANCE *5 miles*

ORDNANCE SURVEY MAPS
1:50,000
Landranger 110 - Sheffield & Huddersfield
1:25,000
Outdoor Leisure 21 - South Pennines

ACCESS *Start from the town centre. Served by bus from Huddersfield, Holmfirth and Oldham; by train from Huddersfield and Manchester.*

Easy walking on a fine selection of old ways, discovering charming cloughs and delightful old settlements of the Colne Valley.

🅢 Slaithwaite is a typical Pennine mill-town, which grew from the establishment of large mills in the boom years of the woollen industry. The earlier mills took advantage of the fast-flowing river and side-streams, while the arrival of the canal in 1798 was a further boost to the local economy. The waterway currently disappears in a culvert for about a quarter-mile across the town centre: it is one of the last sections being restored and should be back in service by 2001, when the canal will once again bring a little prosperity back to the town. Slaithwaite also has the unlikely claim to have been a spa town, after a 19th century hydropathic centre was created upon discovery of a mineral spring. Unlike several other similarly sounding place-names, Slaithwaite is not pronounced as it sounds; but ideally as Sla-wit!

From the crossroads at Britannia Road and Station Road, turn along Market Place, passing the *Shoulder of Mutton* pub and beneath the parish church of St. James. Quickly bear left on Nabbs Lane. The *Silent Woman* pub on the right bears evidence of its former name the

Globe Inn, and its equally defunct brewer, Bentley & Shaw of Lockwood, just three or four miles away on the edge of Huddersfield. **The road then bears right as Holme Lane, rising beneath the tall railway viaduct. A steep climb leads to a path going off right, crossing over the dam of Slaithwaite Reservoir.** Locally known as Hill Top Reservoir, it was constructed to help supply the canal with water.

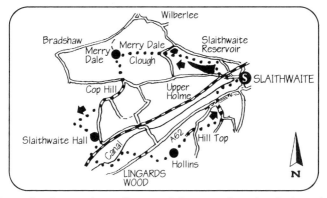

Immediately over the outflow turn left on a well used path along the reservoir bank, with a water cut on the right. This leads increasingly pleasantly into the wooded environs of the reservoir head. Passing a weir at the start of the mill-cut, the lovely environs lead up to the foot of a smaller dam. The water's edge here is a favourite haunt for the heron. **The right of way continues up the broad track onto a road, then goes left the short way to Clough House Bridge on the stream a little higher. However, local preference is to use the path over the smaller dam, and right a short way to cross the outflow above a waterfall tumbling into a small ravine. Then going left to bridge the main stream and resuming right on a public footpath.** In the appropriate season, both bluebells and bilberries decorate this lovely corner. **The path rises to run above the edge of the wooded clough and quickly out onto a road.**

Go right the short way down to Clough House Bridge, immediately over which take a gate on the left and resume upstream into Merry Dale Clough, with the tiny brook for company. Ignoring an early footbridge this is a splendid ramble, a faint path staying close to the tiny stream as it burbles through colourful rough pastures. This remains so for some time until reaching an impasse as a grassy bridge

crosses the stream. Here the path slants to the right, through a cutting and (past a reedy dam on the left) up a snicket and steps by the house at Merry Dale. Continue straight up the path, joining the drive for the final yards onto the setted Tyas Lane, an old packhorse route.

Double back left down this narrow way to a stone arched bridge in wooded Bradshaw Clough. Up the other side it winds steeply up as the narrow bridleway of Scout Lane through heather and bilberry banks to emerge onto a drive. Go straight ahead to reach a crossroads, and straight over on Marsden Lane, quickly passing the pleasant *Rose & Crown* pub at Cop Hill. At about 985ft/300m this is the summit of the walk, with grand views over the valley, notably up-dale to Marsden sheltering beneath its moorland environs.

Keep straight on, ignoring a left turn at Green Lane Farm. After a sharp bend the lane turns downhill, where take the first turn right to a lone house. Pass along the rear and straight on a field bottom. After a stile keep on to another across a tiny stream to arrive at a waterlogged old way descending between the fields. Go left just a matter of yards with it and escape by a stile opposite. Contrastingly steady walking follows the left-hand wall away to a stile overlooking the gorgeous clough in front.

A thin fenceside path descends, becoming stepped to drop onto a level path. The glorious surround of heather, bilberry and birch trees make this a perfect place to linger awhile. Turn left on the inviting path for a steady contour above the deepening wooded clough. The path runs on above its edge on a heathery bank, then bears away from it to approach the settlement ahead. It curves up to a green track which drops down to a gate/stile into the hamlet of Slaithwaite Hall. Go right a short way and then in the centre turn left to follow its short access road back out onto the narrow Marsden Lane.

Drop steeply down just as far as a hairpin bend, then escape on an inviting enclosed way slanting down to the right. In view below are the canal, a millpond behind it and a reservoir in front, with the railway immediately below. Becoming sunken the old way winds down to meet the foot of Netherwood Lane. Go left under the railway out onto Park Gate Road. Just to the left a cart track turns down to Sandhill Cottages, passing Sparth Reservoir on the right. Joining the canal, pass right of the houses on the left to cross the canal by a footbridge. This continues on to another footbridge over a millpond, but instead of crossing it, take a short path left to drop down onto the towpath.

Slaithwaite: the Rose & Crown and parish church

Turning right/east for Slaithwaite, follow the towpath for just a few short minutes as far as a lock. This is a grand corner, with a holding basin immediately above it where barges would queue for the narrow lock, the scene being completed by ducks and a cottage (illustrated on page 85). For the easiest return to Slaithwaite simply follow this back, a grand walk in itself. **Here however take a small gate on the right and a firm path runs down the wallside to a footbridge on the river Colne.** Destined for a rapid entry into a more industrial landscape, the unsung river nevertheless provides a grand moment here. **The path rises away, over a mill-cut with the millpond on the left. It then climbs steps and a fieldside to enter the car park of the *Olive Branch* on the A62 by a bus stop at Lingards Wood.**

Go left on the footway, briefly, passing a crossroads with minor access roads. The building just below explains how School Lane acquired its name. **Just a minute further cross to rise up a setted**

driveway to the right. **At the lodge just ahead, bear right as a rough trackway takes over. At a junction above, bend left on a more inviting way along to the shell of Nathans.** This is a sad specimen of a once fine farmstead-cum-weaving settlement. Of interest is a terrace above two stores with arched roofs beneath the house, with an initialled 1758 datestone between.

From the little gate beyond cross a field bottom to a kissing-gate and tiny stream, then along a field top on a substantially flagged way to approach Hollins Farm. At the gate/stile note the old privy, and on the house itself an initialled 1757 datestone. **Advance straight along the drive, which leads without complication as Hollins Lane onto Lingards Road at Hill Top.** Also known locally as Top o' the Hill this settlement enjoys wide views over the Colne Valley. Just across the road is a former 19th century chapel and school.

Go right a few yards and resume on a grassy way behind a barn. This slants up beneath old grassed over quarry spoil, but is soon left by a fence-stile, with a wall-stile just beyond taking a nice path along a field top. Slaithwaite is now just below, its two viaducts prominent either side of the church. **From a corner stile the thin path resumes above the wall, and on between converging walls to arrive at a cluster of houses at New House. A gate/stile on the right points us past the houses of this historic settlement and out onto a crossroads of narrow back roads.**

Turn left down Yew Tree Lane to descend narrowly and steeply back into Slaithwaite. Go straight down to a crossroads, and slant down the bottom section (Lingards Road) to rejoin the main road. Cross and a few yards to the right take a footpath which winds down steps on a wooded bank to a footbridge on the river Colne. Already the river appears far less seemly than our recent previous crossing. **Bear left of the works buildings to join the canal at a lock just ahead.** This is the unique Lock 23, which has been restored with a vertical 'guillotine' gate now in place, due to widening of the road bridge leaving limited space for a convential lock. **Turn right on the towpath (also used by vehicles) to quickly reach the centre, passing a floating tearoom and a final lock as the canal's current demise also marks that of the walk.**

SCAMMONDEN WATER

START Deanhead   Grid ref. SE 047162

DISTANCE 3½ miles

ORDNANCE SURVEY MAPS
1:50,000
Landranger 110 - Sheffield & Huddersfield
1:25,000
Outdoor Leisure 21 - South Pennines

ACCESS Start from a Yorkshire Water car park just off the B6114 Greetland-Buckstones road (Saddleworth Road) just south of the Brown Cow, south of the M62 bridge. Buses from Halifax via Ripponden.

An easy circuit of Scammonden Water, with a good range of views.

S The M62 trans-Pennine motorway was first conceived in 1961, and ten years later traffic was tracing its graceful lines over the Yorkshire-Lancashire watershed. In between, men and machinery laboured through the Pennine weather, hampered by some rough winters. The engineering achievement that earned greatest recognition was the bridging of the Scammonden valley, a project that took over three years to complete. It so happened that a reservoir had been planned around the same time, and logical consensus was that the two could combine to serve each other's needs. Thus it was that a larger than initially conceived dam, some 249ft high, would span the valley and carry the motorway towards its summit goal four miles to the west.

The walk's starting point overlooks the grassy dam of the reservoir and its motorway crossing. **From the car park take the no-through-road towards the dam, bending right at a lone white house and running on to the old Deanhead church just ahead.** Scammonden Water glistens below, with its sailing club on the opposite shore. The little hamlet of Deanhead still has several dwellings, including the former school. The church is a Victorian replacement of an earlier building.

Pass to the right of the old school on a grassy track running on above the church. Just above are the gritstone cliffs of Scar Rocks. **At the end of the churchyard is a fork. Bear left, a splendid path angling gently down through trees and then running a level course along the colourful bank, with the upper section of the reservoir below.** High on the skyline is the *Nont Sarah's* pub, while straight ahead is our objective of the grassy embankment of Deanhead Reservoir.

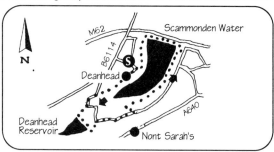

The path runs on, dropping a little to a stile in a fence and thence to a fork above the very reservoir head. The lower path is just below, parallel, and it joins the main lower branch just ahead. Our route takes the upper fork, rising a few feet to run along the top side of a crumbling wall along the base of a bilberry bank. At the end the faint path crosses the wall and joins New Lane at the top of a small wood. Resume along the road down to a hairpin bend, then go straight ahead to a gate/stile, and a grassy track runs on to the end of the embankment of Deanhead Reservoir.** An information board advises that we are within a Site of Special Scientific Interest, an important breeding site for a variety of birds who favour this habitat.

A stile gives access to the grassy dam top. Deanhead Reservoir was completed in 1836 to supply textile mills. Down valley is Scammonden Water, revealing the motorway by the time the far side is reached. Across this upper reservoir, the cloughs and folds of Deanhead Moor present a much wilder scene, true rough Pennine slopes. Note the criss-cross of field walls on the northern slopes, not an intact wall among them as water interests ensured farming took a back seat.

Having bridged the outflow take the rough road (a permissive path not on older maps) down onto New Lane, and turn right on this as it climbs then levels out as Sledge Gate. On reaching a sailing club/activity centre drive on the left, turn down it, soon doubling back to run on to the club and the outdoor centre. Here the path is sent off to the right, rising around the top of the grounds by a small footbridge and on to a fork at the foot of a walled green way. Bear left to a stile, the firm path running on above the sailing clubhouse in the old vicarage, and then down almost to the water's edge.

Now it is a simple case of following the reservoir-side path towards the motorway. The mixed woodland and heather of the adjacent slopes are a welcome distraction from the animated sight just ahead. An access road is reached by the valve tower at the end. A tablet proclaims Scammonden Water's official opening by Her Majesty the Queen on 14th October 1971, while the turning circle has the points of the compass inset. Although people regularly cross the dam by a path visible above the waterline, the official route turns up the path on the right, then branches off level to the end of the embankment. The dam is thus crossed just a fence away from the waggons.

At the far end don't follow the surfaced track up onto a road, but drop left, past an underpass entrance and along an initially thin path through the mixed vegetation of the colourful bank. This soon improves into a lovely walk at mid height above the shoreline. Reaching a guidepost at the start of a small plantation, a thin path climbs the steep little bank on the right: the house seen above is the white house at the start of the walk. A stile admits onto the road bend, though another just above admits directly into the picnic area.

Deanhead Church

LOG OF THE WALKS

WALK	DATE	NOTES
1		
2		
3		
4		
5		
6		
7		
8		
9		
10		
11		
12		
13		
14		
15		
16		
17		
18		
19		
20		
21		
22		

SOME USEFUL ADDRESSES

Ramblers' Association   1/5 Wandsworth Road, London SW8 2XX
Tel. 0171-339 8500

Information Centres
Brownhill Countryside Centre **Dobcross** Tel. 01457-872598
Hollingworth Lake Littleborough Tel. 01706-373421
49-51 Huddersfield Road **Holmfirth** Tel. 01484-222444
High Street Buildings, Albion Street **Huddersfield** Tel. 01484-223200
The Coach House **Littleborough** Tel. 01706-378481
Tunnel End **Marsden** Tel. 01484-846062
Tommyfield Market Hall **Oldham** Tel. 0161-627 1024
Saddleworth Museum **Uppermill** Tel. 01457-870336

Peak District National Park Visitor Services
Aldern House, Baslow Road, Bakewell, Derbyshire DE45 1AE
Tel. 01629-816200

Yorkshire Tourist Board
312 Tadcaster Road, York YO2 2HF
Tel. 01904-707961

North West Tourist Board
Swan House, Swan Meadow Road, Wigan Pier, Wigan WN3 5BB
Tel. 01942-821222

The National Trust Marsden Moor Estate Office
The Old Goods Yard, Station Rd, Marsden, Huddersfield HD7 6DH
Tel. 01484-847016

Huddersfield Canal Society
239 Mossley Road, Ashton-under-Lyne OL6 6LN
Tel. 0161-339 1332

Greater Manchester Passenger Transport Executive
9 Portland Street, Piccadilly Gardens, Manchester M60 1HX
Tel. 0161-228 7811

Metro (West Yorkshire buses and trains) Tel. 0113-245 7676

Rail services - National Enquiry Line   Tel. 0345-484950

INDEX
Principal features (walk number refers)